# Making Mentoring Work

### Emily Davis

ROWMAN & LITTLEFIELD
*Lanham • Boulder • New York • London*

Text content from Chapter 3 originally appeared in Betty Achinstein and Emily Davis, "The Subject of Mentoring: Towards a Knowledge and Practice Base for Content-focused Mentoring of New Teachers," *Mentoring & Tutoring: Partnership in Learning* 22, no. 2 (pp. 104–26). For additional information please visit www.tandfonline.com.

Published by Rowman & Littlefield Education
A division of Rowman & Littlefield Publishers, Inc.
A wholly owned subsidiary of The Rowman & Littlefield Publishing Group, Inc.
4501 Forbes Boulevard, Suite 200, Lanham, Maryland 20706
www.rowman.com

10 Thornbury Road, Plymouth PL6 7PP, United Kingdom

British Library Cataloguing in Publication Information Available

**Library of Congress Cataloging-in-Publication Data**
Davis, Emily, 1978 December 10–
    Making mentoring work / Emily Davis.
        pages cm
    Includes bibliographical references.
    ISBN 978-1-4758-0409-6 (cloth : alk. paper) — ISBN 978-1-4758-0410-2 (pbk. : alk. paper) — ISBN 978-1-4758-0411-9 (electronic)
    1. Mentoring in education.    2. First year teachers.    I. Title.
    LB1731.4D38 2014
    371.102—dc23

                                                                2014022895

♾ ™ The paper used in this publication meets the minimum requirements of American National Standard for Information Sciences—Permanence of Paper for Printed Library Materials, ANSI/NISO Z39.48-1992.

Printed in the United States of America

# OTHER RLE TITLES ON EDUCATIONAL MENTORING

*Stopping the Brain Drain of Skilled Veteran Teachers: Retaining and Valuing their Hard-Won Experience* by William L. Fibkins

*A Life Saver for New Teachers: Mentoring Case Studies to Navigate the Initial Years* by Richard E. Lange

*An Administrator's Guide to Better Teacher Mentoring–2nd Edition* by William L. Fibkins

*Mentoring the Educational Leader: A Practical Framework for Success* by Kimberly T. Strike and John Nickelsen

*Mentoring Matters: A Toolkit for Organizing and Operating Student Advisory Programs* by Mark Benigni and Sheryll Petrosky

*The Faculty Mentor's Wisdom: Conceptualizing, Writing, and Defending the Dissertation* Edited by Raymond L. Calabrese and Page Smith

# Contents

*Contents*

# List of Figures, Tables, and Textboxes

# Foreword

Teacher effectiveness has been shown to be the single most important school-based indicator of student success. Effective teachers can offset—even eliminate—the disadvantage of a low socioeconomic background. Schools with high populations of students living in poverty typically have the lowest academic achievement (based on state test scores) and lowest high school graduation rates. Beyond those challenged by poverty and social status, many more students across the country are also at a disadvantage due to stressful life events that negatively influence their behavior and learning habits, ultimately thwarting success in school and happiness in life.

To break the cycle of inequity in our education system, schools everywhere need highly effective teachers. Yet the most challenging classroom environments are in the schools most likely to be assigned beginning, inexperienced teachers. A new teacher's first few years in the classroom are difficult in any school setting, but the unique challenge of teaching in a high-needs school is especially daunting.

Great teachers are made, not born. Yet, when new teachers are placed in these challenging classroom environments, they often are abandoned to "sink or swim" on their own. Too often, they become discouraged and leave the profession before they become effective. Nearly 50 percent of all new teachers leave the profession within five years. This number is even higher in underserved environments.

This revolving door costs U.S schools over $7 billion annually—money that could otherwise be invested in the human capital development of educators. And it's not just about money. The high teacher turnover rate saps schools of talent and messages to students that it's okay to leave school. Each year, approximately 15.2 million of our nation's students in high-poverty schools pay the price of a less effective new teacher at the front of their classroom. This trial-by-fire of our novice educators in our most disadvantaged schools fuels the cycle of inequity and deepens the crisis in our nation's education system.

I saw this phenomenon first-hand when I was the Director of Teacher Education at the University of California–Santa Cruz (UCSC). I had so many bright, passionate students who I knew would make great teachers. I was so excited when they graduated and started their first teaching jobs. But by October of their first year, these same students who previously showed so much promise and excitement would come back to me saying, "I can't do this," "I don't think I'm meant to be a teacher," and "I want to quit." And it wasn't the students who barely graduated from the education program who were saying this. It was my star students—the ones who had the potential to have the greatest impact on kids. It crushed me.

I knew there had to be some way to support these new teachers through their first years on the job so that they could get better faster and stay in the classroom longer. Through UCSC, I piloted an intensive, instructional-based mentoring program that ultimately became what New Teacher Center is today. We paired carefully selected, rigorously trained mentors with a small caseload of new teachers. They worked together one-on-one every week for two years. The results were incredible. The new teachers were getting on the path to excellence early in their careers, they were staying longer in the classroom, and their students were learning more. It was also great for the mentors, who were reinvigorated by the professional development and leadership opportunity this gave them.

Over time, we honed our model and learned more about the systemic supports new teachers need in order to maximize their potential as educators. We built things like school leader support, school district capacity building support, and impact assessment into our model. We know that teaching and learning conditions within a school are critical, so we assess those conditions and work with school, district, and state leaders to ensure they are creating the best learning environment for their teachers and students.

To be its most successful, this work can't happen in a vacuum. We take a nested approach to our work, where we are modeling the same kind of learning experience with our mentors and principals that we want them to model with their new teachers and that we want teachers to use with their students. Where we've taken this approach, educators at all levels of the system work from a shared understanding and common language for teaching and learning. This work transforms the culture of teaching and learning across a district.

One of the important points in this book is that new teacher induction is more than a mentoring program—even a strong one. Now, we know what it takes to have a strong induction *system* for new teachers. We know how to situate new teacher induction within a larger human capital development system in order to build, maintain, and sustain excellent educators and students who thrive. Dr. Emily Davis' passion and expertise in building comprehensive induction systems that impact teaching and learning provide a solid foundation for this book.

Just as new teachers need support in translating their knowledge into practice, districts need support in translating the theories of new teacher support into a sustainable induction system. And just as self-reflection is an important process for the continuous improvement of any educator, the rubric can be a powerful step in the continuous improvement of any induction system. The practical design of this book supports the implementation of an induction system and allows opportunities for any education agency to improve how it develops new teachers and improves student learning.

The growing national dialogue and focus on education reform increasingly advocates for improving the effectiveness of teacher practice and supports increased teacher training and mentoring. This trend, along with implementation of Common Core State Standards in over forty states, and increased recognition of the need for social and emotional learning to support academic success, will prove the value of great professional development for teachers. There has never been a more critical time to advance the knowledge and expertise of those responsible for advancing teacher practice in these areas. Investing in high-quality teacher induction and support for new teachers and school leaders represents the greatest opportunity to affect change in the educational opportunities for kids today.

—Ellen Moir
Founder and CEO of the New Teacher Center

# Preface

$M$aking Mentoring Work is a step-by-step guide to building or transforming your new teacher mentoring program into a powerful component of a comprehensive induction system. Using the ideas and tools provided by this book, leaders can create a mentoring program tailored to meet the needs and context of their schools. By creating such a program, schools and districts will be able to improve teacher retention and accelerate the development of new teachers so all students have access to the high-quality teachers they deserve.

By reading this book, the assumption is that you already know the value of mentoring and induction for new teachers and have made the decision to implement a program in your school or district to support new teachers during the early phase of their careers. Understanding why mentoring works and what makes it successful is a complicated topic. The introduction to this book explores the value of creating mentoring programs for new teachers, describes the components of effective mentoring programs, the difference between induction and mentoring, and explains why mentors are important but not enough to truly support new teachers. It ends with a discussion on mentoring and the components of effective mentoring programs. This information will provide you with valuable background knowledge and research that may prove useful should you be asked to justify the development and/or continuation of your program by your principal, superintendent, or school board.

Even with this information, however, starting and running a successful mentoring program is a complicated endeavor with many unforeseen potential pitfalls. If you are just starting a mentoring program, this book will help you consider a set of issues that often cause mentoring programs to be less than successful but that are often overlooked when such programs are organized. By addressing these issues, you can tailor your mentoring program to make mentoring work better for new teachers and, by extension, the district, school, and students who work with them.

If there is already a mentoring program in your school or district, this book will help you identify challenges, fine-tune your program, and engage in a process of continuous improvement. By taking a systematic look at your program, this book will reinforce what is already going well, highlight areas for growth, locate barriers to success, and help you determine the appropriate research-based steps to correct or avoid the pitfalls that, when left unaddressed, can cause mentoring programs to flounder.

So how does this book work? Prior to making any adjustments to your program, it is vital to assess the current state of your induction program. After reading the introduction, begin by using the New Teacher Mentoring Program Assessment Rubric to self-assess your program and determine current levels of practice.

After assessing your program, you can choose how best to use the remaining three sections of the book to meet your program's needs. These three sections align to the three domains of the rubric, and each section contains chapters that match the elements of each domain. You can either read through the whole book to learn about all of the rubric domains, or you can pick and choose the chapters that are most relevant to the needs of your program and schools, based on your self-assessment. This setup is intended to ensure that you can quickly access the research, best practices, and tools necessary to give your mentoring program a strong start, or to tighten a few practices and processes in order to make your program truly successful.

If you are ready to become a savvy leader of your school or district's mentoring initiative who

- makes sound choices about mentor selection, development, and deployment,
- provides an adaptable program that takes into account the needs and strengths of new teachers,
- understands the need to coordinate with school leaders to create a seamless pipeline of new teacher support in order to reduce costly teacher turnover and improve the quality of teaching and learning for your district, schools, and students,

then *Making Mentoring Work* will show you where to start.

# Acknowledgments

I have the great fortune to spend my days with incredibly talented, dedicated, and smart people who live and breathe the ideas in this book every day as both researchers and practitioners. I have learned so much from all of you, and I am extremely thankful for that. Laura Gschwend and Steve Sinclair, thank you for your support and amazing leadership in our project each and every day and for your constant support and thoughtful feedback. To Fred Williams, Josh Maisel, and Kim Ortiz for sharing your own experiences and resources as program directors as well as for taking the time to read and make this book better through your contributions. Ellen Moir, Wendy Baron, Betty Achinstein, and Michael Strong, I stand on your shoulders. This work would not have been possible without the groundwork you provided as well as your friendship and encouragement. Above all, I want to thank my husband, Jason, who supported and encouraged me even though writing this book took away from spending time with our family.

# Introduction

## Planning for New Teacher Success: An Exploration of Best Practices

This chapter explores the value of creating mentoring programs for new teachers, describes the components of effective mentoring programs, the difference between induction and mentoring, and explains why mentors are important but not enough to truly support new teachers. It ends with a discussion of mentoring and the components of effective mentoring programs.

Teaching is hard work, and it takes a great deal of time, energy, and dedication to learn how to do it well. The relatively short period of preservice training teachers traditionally receive from their university and through student teaching experiences is rarely sufficient to provide all the knowledge and skills necessary to ensure a teacher will be successful. For future teachers who enter the profession through alternative routes, the training and support is even more inadequate.

Other professions, such as doctors and lawyers, recognize that introductory coursework is not enough to ensure success and, therefore, provide on-the-job training for those newest to their fields. Physicians go through multiple years and stages of residency, and new law associates often go through training developed by their law firms. Both professions require years of gradual release before they are allowed to work on patients or cases independently.

Yet while no one would think to allow a first-year surgical resident to perform a solo surgery, our newest teachers are regularly left alone with an incomplete knowledge and skill set to "sink or swim" in their first years of teaching; too often, they leave the learning of youngsters hanging in the balance.

1

Like novice doctors, lawyers, and other professionals, structured opportunities for new teachers to continue developing their professional knowledge and skills for continued learning are crucial. In the last twenty-five years, mentoring programs for teachers have become the dominant form of teacher induction and have begun to fill this need in the teaching profession. In fact, mentoring has become so integral to most new teacher induction programs that the terms *induction* and *mentoring* are often mistakenly used interchangeably.

While most readers of this book are well aware of the positive impact of induction and mentoring programs for new teachers, it may be valuable to consider why these programs were originally created, the needs they fill, and the value they add to schools, teachers, and students.

## WORTH THE INVESTMENT:
## MAKING A CASE FOR NEW TEACHER INDUCTION

Over the last twenty-five years, the teaching population has changed dramatically. In 1987, a student in the United States was most likely to be assigned to a fifteen-year veteran. Today, there are more first-year teachers in U.S. classrooms than teachers with any other experience level.[1] The number of new teachers entering the classroom is not going down any time soon, either. By some estimates, U.S. schools will need to hire two million new teachers by 2020.[2] This dramatic change in workforce creates teacher shortages across the country that causes schools to be unable to ensure a quality teacher for every student.

Despite popular opinion, the teacher shortage crisis does not stem from a lack of teachers entering the profession. Since the early 1980s, teacher education programs—both traditional and alternative—have churned out new teachers at a rate that should far exceed the number of open teaching positions across the country each year. Yet despite the large number of new teachers entering the profession, there continues to be a shortfall of qualified teachers, particularly in high-need subject areas (i.e., math, science, and special education). In the last decade or so, the shortage, particularly in these areas, has become critical. How is this possible with so many teachers entering the profession each year? It turns out that it is not the number of new teachers entering the profession that is causing the shortage; rather, it is the rapid exit of quality teachers from the profession.

Studies have found that half of all urban teachers in the United States leave the profession within their first three to five years.[3] In urban school districts like Philadelphia's, the turnover rate is closer to 70 percent. Even more startling, a recent study from The New Teacher Project indicates that it is often the highest achieving and most effective new teachers that leave within the first five years.[4]

The authors of the 2003 National Commission on Teaching and America's Future report *No Dream Denied: A Pledge to America's Children*, observe, "The real school staffing problem is teacher retention. Our inability to support high quality teaching in many of our schools is driven not by too few teachers entering the profession, but by too many leaving it for other jobs. Clearly, teacher retention has become a national crisis."[5]

The failure to retain high-quality teachers in schools is troublesome for education in part because it is costly in terms of teacher effectiveness, finances, and student learning. While some turnover is expected and even healthy, a high level of employee turnover in any organization is "both cause and effect of ineffectiveness and low performance in organizations."[6] Unfortunately, the turnover in education is significantly higher than in other professions. In 2001, the annual turnover for all nonteaching occupations was 11 percent while the annual rate was nearly 16 percent for education.[7] Some teachers leave the classroom due to promotions such as a move to administration, while other leave due to a desire to increase their salary; because they feel unsupported by their administration; underprepared to teach, particularly in more challenging schools; or for family-related issues.

Whatever the reason for the departure from the classroom, high turnover is costly. A study in Texas estimated the cost of teacher turnover at a staggering $329 million per year, or approximately $8,000 per teacher, which means that districts spend approximately 20 to 200 percent of the leaving teacher's annual salary to replace her.[8] In 2007, the National Commission on Teaching and America's Future placed the cost of teacher turnover in the United States at over $7.3 billion annually.

How is this money being spent? School districts spend significant money each time they recruit and train new teachers, and those funds are lost when teachers leave the district. Constant recruitment and training of new teachers means districts must spend precious resources on hiring and training instead of on building an experienced and high-quality workforce.

Above and beyond the fiscal consequences, teacher quality also has a huge impact on students' academic achievement.[9] Researchers, including Linda Darling-Hammond, have shown again and again that students who are assigned to several ineffective teachers in a row have significantly lower achievement and slower gains in achievement than those students assigned to a sequence of several highly effective teachers. They have also reported that inexperienced teachers—those with fewer than three years of experience—were typically less effective at making changes in students than their veteran counterparts. And even if teachers stay beyond their first few years, it takes several more years to reach the proficiency and quality demonstrated by expert teachers.

While novice teachers may eventually grow toward proficiency on their own, the learning curve is steep:

> If we leave beginning teachers to sink or swim on their own, they may become overwhelmed and leave the field. Alternatively, they may stay, clinging to practices and attitudes that help them to survive but do not serve the educational needs of students. A high quality induction program should increase the probability that new teachers learn desirable lessons from their early teaching experiences.[10]

For all of the reasons described above, induction and, particularly, mentoring, has become a tremendously popular way of retaining and supporting new teachers—and it seems to be working. In study after study, researchers find that beginning teachers who received some type of induction had higher job satisfaction, efficacy, success, and retention than those who received no structured support in their early years of teaching.

Studies have shown that providing novice teachers with quality induction programs, which include mentoring, may mitigate the teacher-attrition and teacher-staffing issues now facing many school districts in the United States, particularly high-need schools. A 1999 study conducted in California of seventy-two teachers who were enrolled in the Santa Cruz New Teacher Project mentoring program found 88 percent of those who received mentoring support were still in the classroom six years later; in contrast, only about 50 percent of teachers from neighboring districts who were not receiving mentoring were still in the classroom.[11]

There is also growing evidence that novice teachers who are provided with comprehensive induction support for two years are more likely to have classes that achieve at rates similar to those of veteran teachers rather than their nonmentored new teacher peers.[12] The positive outcomes for student achievement as well as for growth in teacher learning and practice seem to be more fully achieved when the novice teacher is paired with a highly trained mentor who is knowledgeable about his or her subject or grade level.[13] For example, a federally funded, randomized, controlled trial found that beginning teachers who received two years of induction produced greater student-learning gains when compared with those who received less intensive mentoring. The gains were equivalent to a student going from the fiftieth to the fifty-eighth percentile in math and from fiftieth to the fifty-fourth percentile in reading.[14]

In addition to gains in student test scores, researchers are also finding that teachers who receive intensive mentoring persist in using high-quality teaching practices long beyond their nonmentored peers. Julie Luft's 2009 study of induction programs for new science teachers found that science-specific induction helps new teachers continue building and solidifying their disciplinary (e.g., general science, biology, chemistry) and topic (e.g., heat, motion) pedagogical content knowledge, and they persist in practices consistent with National Science Education Standards throughout their careers. Persisting in these practices that have been proven to be powerful for student learning, instead of reverting to text-book-driven or other less effective methods of instruction, means that students are benefitting from working with new teachers even though those teachers have less experience and, therefore, students are experiencing learning gains far beyond what they might have without the support of the mentor.

Moreover, the positive effects of induction and mentoring seem to hold true in both high-poverty and high-minority-enrollment schools and across all levels of schooling from elementary to high school.[15] As a result of this kind of research, almost every state now offers at least some form of induction support for new teachers. One study posits that approximately 75 percent of novice teachers receive some form of induction support today. With the inclusion of induction in most of the successful Race to the Top grant applications, the number continues to grow.

The early career phase of teaching represents a critical time for teacher retention and development as well as for student learning and is where savvy schools and districts are investing significant resources to ensure teachers stay, grow, and can have positive impact on students.

## TAILORING SUPPORT TO MEET
## NEW TEACHER NEEDS

Creating a program that includes a high-quality mentor is an important first step in the development of school or district supports for new teachers. However, it is not the only step that should be taken to increase satisfaction and retention levels for novice teachers and, through them, boost student learning. While having a mentor is an important first step, the mere presence of a mentor is not enough to ensure a new teacher's success. Mentoring programs also need to be able to tailor their programs to meet the needs of new teachers who enter the profession from diverse backgrounds and with a wide range of professional experiences, readiness, and sense of efficacy. Some already have advanced degrees in the content area they plan to teach, attended high-quality teacher preparation programs, and have chosen teaching positions that align with those experiences. Some have previous real-world experiences that lend themselves to teaching. Some do not. The wide array of variables that impact a novices' experience as they begin teaching means that they need different things to grow.

Consider, for example, these three new teachers:

Diane is a first-year high school chemistry teacher in an urban district. She has an undergraduate degree in biology and, as a part of her teacher residency program, she was an intern teacher in a biology classroom. She generally feels well prepared to teach biology—but not chemistry. In addition, she has found that her alternative urban school differs dramatically from the suburban school where she did her student teaching.

Jerome has recently accepted a kindergarten position at the elementary school where he student taught during his university teacher preparation program. Having previously taught in this school as a teacher candidate means he knows many of the teachers in the school and has a strong support network. However, during his student teaching, he worked only in third- and fourth-grade classes, which leaves him feeling unprepared to work with students this young. He is struggling to figure out how to handle the developmental needs of four- and five-year-olds and how to deal with anxious parents.

Tamako spent the last ten years working in the business world and has recently decided to make a career change. She has accepted a position as a middle school math teacher on an emergency credential and is taking classes at night toward a teaching degree. She has a great deal of real-world knowledge to bring to her role, but having never student taught, she has little experience with classroom management, curriculum development, and the needs of young adolescents.

Would the same mentor be appropriate for all three of these teachers with their vastly different backgrounds, preparation, and current contexts? Imagine, for example, that the same experienced high school English teacher was assigned to mentor all of these new teachers. No matter how well prepared, she might not be able to provide the content support or the age-specific instructional knowledge that each of these teachers would need to succeed.

Yet despite the differences in these teachers' situations, mentoring programs all too often offer them the same kind of support. Some simply pair new teachers with a veteran "buddy" in the building who may or may not have experience teaching the same grade or content as the novice. This buddy may have little training and no release time to support the novice. Other programs hire a veteran teacher to support all of the new teachers in a school or district. Although these "full-release mentors"—those whose full-time job is to provide mentoring to novice teachers—are often considered high-quality educators and who often receive training to be mentors, they often have heavy caseloads and are asked to support novice teachers in a wide range of contexts and content areas with whom they may not be knowledgeable.

## CREATING A PROFESSIONAL LADDER
## WITHIN THE CLASSROOM

Creating a mentoring program has other benefits for teachers, schools, and districts beyond supporting new teachers. Schools and districts who have mentoring programs in place say that the experience of learning to mentor is particularly helpful at renewing passion and drive in veteran teachers, building high-quality teacher leaders, and retaining these highly knowledgeable and skilled educators in the profession.

Research has long documented that most teachers enter the profession because they want to positively influence the lives of students.[16] Pursuing teaching as a way to positively affect individuals and society is particularly apparent in the new generation of teachers (those with ten years of experience or fewer), who now make up the majority of teachers in the United States.[17] They love working with students, but they also have a commitment to social justice and believe that teaching can improve society on a broader scale.[18]

Many great teachers leave in their early years because they want to find a way to have more impact on the broader system, and they find it challenging to do so from within a classroom. Although a recent poll found that only about 16 percent of teachers want to become administrators (one of the few career moves teachers have), more than 50 percent said they would be interested in finding ways to combine teaching with other leadership roles such as department chair or mentoring.[19]

Keeping good teachers requires the education profession to offer career ladders or career jungle gyms[20] that provide teachers the opportunity to stay in their classrooms, grow their leadership skills, and have a positive impact on the system. Mentoring can provide a step in this important career path.

Mentoring allows a teacher to, for a specified period of time, step out of their classrooms either partially or fully, to support other teachers, and to learn and grow their skills in other areas. Schools and districts that have high-quality mentoring programs note that mentor training and experience is the best teacher-leadership program they have ever seen. Learning to mentor new teachers provides these veteran educators with new leadership, organization, communication, and collaboration skills. It also supports them in developing a deeper understanding and belief about what effective teaching and learning looks like and what it takes to help all students succeed.

When mentors have completed their terms, or when they are ready to leave the program, the experiences and skills they learned during their time are highly transferable to other situations. If they choose to return to the classroom, they are much more knowledgeable about effective teaching and learning practices. They also share their new perspectives and knowledge with their colleagues and use their mentoring skills to support their peers in their grade level or school.

Many mentors choose to take their new skills into other leadership roles such as instructional coaching, school leadership, or district positions. Having former mentors serving as school administrators, for example, means that new teachers and current mentors have the benefit of working with principals who are knowledgeable about the needs of new teachers and who can use their skills to coach and grow whole staffs.

The benefits of mentoring described here, which extend beyond the development of new teachers, are valuable for entire schools and systems and add great value to all parts of a school or district beyond new teacher support and retention.

## PACKAGING SUCCESS: WHY A MENTOR ALONE IS NOT ENOUGH

The statistics about induction as a successful strategy for supporting new teachers seem to be overwhelmingly positive. What these statistics don't do, however, is delineate between mentoring as an induction strategy and the larger concept of induction.

As mentioned before, there is much confusion over and misuse of the terms *mentoring* and *induction*. The two terms are not synonymous, though they are often used interchangeably in the literature. *Induction* is a process of comprehensive, coherent, and sustained professional development organized by a school or district to train, support, and retain new teachers and seamlessly progress them into a lifelong learning program. *Mentoring* is an action undertaken by a single person, whose basic function is to help a new teacher.

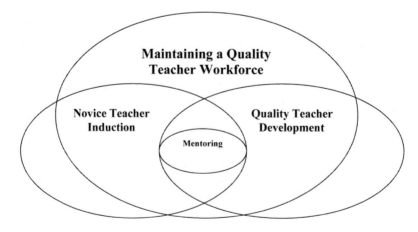

Interconnection Between Mentoring, Induction, Teacher Development, and Workforce Quality

Mentoring is not induction, though a mentor should be a component of the induction process. The problem with many schools and districts is that mentors are offered as the sole means of support for new teachers, and these mentors are not part of a mentoring program, much less a comprehensive induction program.

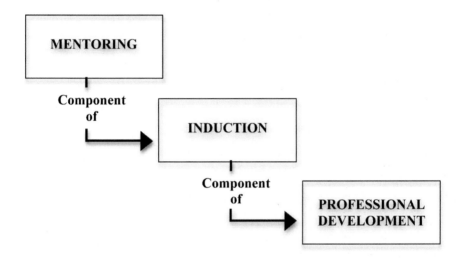

Mentoring, Induction, and Professional Development Relationship
(*Source*: H. Wong, Induction Programs That Keep New Teachers Teaching and Improving, *NASSP Bulletin 88* (638) March 2004.)

So if mentoring alone does not make an induction program, what does a successful induction program include? Numerous studies as well as anecdotal reports suggest there is significant variation in the structure, activity type, duration, and intensity of the support provided to new teachers. Induction programs range from weak support—such as offering a new teacher orientation at the start of the school year and, perhaps, a "buddy mentor"—to strong support—such as a set of differentiated and graduated support options lasting two or more years and including a fully trained content- or grade-specific mentor. What makes an induction program succeed?

In 2003, Richard Ingersoll and Thomas Smith conducted an analysis of two national teacher surveys to determine if there was any relationship between new teacher retention and specific induction activities. What they found was that no single induction program activity by itself made a statistically significant difference on teacher turnover, though some, such as mentoring, were more significant than others. However, what they did find was that the collective impact of receiving several supports or "packages of support" did seem significant.

To learn more, the researchers tested the effects of these packages on retention. They found that as the number of components in the packages increased, the probability of teacher turnover decreased. The biggest impact was seen in the group of teachers who were receiving the most comprehensive package of supports wherein the probability of a departure at the end of the first year was less than half that of those who participated in no induction activities.

Smith and Ingersoll suggest that the most effective package of supports include

- a mentor who is knowledgeable about the novice's subject matter
- common planning time with other teachers in the same grade or subject
- regularly scheduled collaboration with other teachers

Surprisingly, the least robust supports were the things that are often more difficult and costly to implement, such as a reduced teaching schedule or number of preparations, or providing extra classroom assistance. The researchers summed up their findings, writing:

The results indicate that beginning teachers who were provided with mentors from the same subject field and who participated in collective induction activities, such as planning and collaboration with other teachers, were less likely to move to other schools and less likely to leave the teaching occupation after their first year of teaching. While some of the components of induction we examined did not, individually, have a statistically significant impact on teacher turnover, most did collectively. That is, teachers participating in a combination or packages of mentoring and group induction activities were far less likely to depart their jobs at the end of their first year.

The New Teacher Center founder and chief executive officer Ellen Moir reiterated this concept of a package of supports being necessary for new teacher success during a speech at the 2013 Annual New Teacher Center Induction Symposium. She stated that a high-quality mentor is important to support new teachers, but it is not enough. Building on Smith and Ingersoll's insights, she points out that a school leader who knows how to shape a school climate to support new teacher learning and development is important but is not enough. A system that creates the structure for new teacher excellence is also necessary. All of these pieces, by themselves, are important, but all need to be in place to shape new teacher excellence (see figure below).

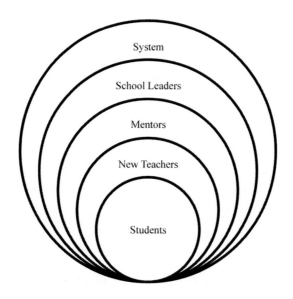

Levels of Support for New Teachers
(*Source*: Moir (2013), Keynote Address to the Annual New Teacher Symposium, San Jose, CA.)

So what does this mean for schools interested in providing high-quality induction for new teachers? For one, it means that support needs to be provided in a number of forms from a number of different people—a mentor, a grade level or subject team, and from the broader school or district community. It also means that there needs to be a schoolwide or districtwide vision of what new teachers need so that new teachers are offered a comprehensive and integrated set of supports at all levels of the organization.

The value of these systems of support within the broader context of *induction* is that they help novices to connect with the organization and develop a wider professional network with others both inside and beyond their school or district that will be able to help them continue learning, growing, and updating their practice throughout their careers, *long after mentor supports have phased out of their working lives*. These various connections should not be underestimated since it is strong connections with colleagues that convince new teachers to stay in teaching and in their schools even when they are considering giving up.

The creation of a comprehensive induction and professional development program should be a goal of a school or district that wishes to attract, retain, and grow its educators. As one program leader put it:

> We realized that we can have a tremendous effect on the learning of thousands of students by investing in our teachers from the beginning. By investing in a comprehensive mentoring, induction, and professional development program, we are making sure to put our funds into what we know works.

Developing such a program takes time, coordination, and strategic decision making on many levels. It requires developing a comprehensive package of supports that includes effective mentors, flexible support structures, and support from site administrators.

This book is designed to help schools and districts to begin the process of creating a comprehensive program of support for new teachers by focusing on the development of a successful mentoring program. It focuses on mentoring because mentors and the process and structures around them are arguably the most important component of a successful induction program. But, again, to be truly successful, mentors must be part of an induction process aligned to the district's vision, mission, and structure. For a mentor to be effective, the mentor must be used in combination with the other components of the induction process.

## NOTES

1. Richard Ingersoll and Lisa Merrill, "Seven Trends: The Transformation of the Teaching Force." Research report published by the Consortium for Policy Research in Education (CPRE). Accessed from: http://www.cpre.org/7trends.

2. National Commission on Teaching & America's Future, "Who Will Teach? Experience Matters." Washington, DC: Author, 2010. Accessed from: http://nctaf .org/teacher-turnover-cost-calculator/who-will-teach-experience-matters/.

3. National Center for Education Statistics, "The Condition of Education 2008." Washington, DC: Author, 2008. Accessed from: nces.ed.gov/pubs2008/2008031 .pdf.

4. Eric Hirsch, Cross-State Analyses of Results of 2012–13 Teaching Empowering Leading and Learning (TELL) Survey Research Report. New Teacher Center. Accessed from: http://www.newteachercenter.org/products-and-resources/teach ing-and-learning-conditions-reports/cross-state-analyses-results-2012-13.

5. National Commission on Teaching and America's Future. "No Dream Denied: A Pledge to America's Children" Washington, D.C. Author, 2003, pg. 8.

6. Richard Ingersoll and T. Smith, "Do Teacher Induction and Mentoring Matter?" *NASSP Bulletin* 88, no. 638 (2004): 28–40.

7. Richard M. Ingersoll, "The Teacher Shortage: A Case of Wrong Diagnosis and Wrong Prescription." *NASSP Bulletin* 86, no. 631 (2002): 16–31.

8. Edward J. Fuller, "Do Properly Certified Teachers Matter? Properly Certified Algebra Teachers and Algebra I Achievement in Texas." Paper presented at the Annual Meeting of the American Educational Research Association, New Orleans, Louisiana; M. S. Norton, "Teacher Retention: Reducing Costly Turnover." *Contemporary Education* 70, no. 3 (1999): 52–55.

9. Mark Teoh and Celine Coggins, "Great Expectations: Teachers' Views on Elevating the Teaching Profession." Boston: Teach Plus, 2013. Accessed from: www.teachplus.org/.

10. Sharon Feiman-Nemser, "What New Teachers Need to Learn." *Educational Leadership* 60, no. 8 (2003): 25–29.

11. Michael Strong and Linda St. John, *A Study of Teacher Retention: The Effects of Mentoring for Beginning Teachers.* Santa Cruz, CA: New Teacher Center, 2001.

12. Michael Strong, "Does New Teacher Support Affect Student Achievement?" *Research Brief* 06, no. 1 (2006).

13. Donald J. Boyd, Pam Grossman, Hamilton Lankford, Susanna Loeb, Matthew Ronfeldt, and Jim Wyckoff, "Recruiting Effective Math Teachers: Evidence From New York City." *American Educational Research Journal* 49, no. 6 (2012): 1008–47; Jonah E. Rockoff, "Does Mentoring Reduce Turnover and Improve Skills of New Employees? Evidence from Teachers in New York City" (Working Paper 13868). Cambridge, MA: National Bureau of Economic Research, 2008. Accessed from: www.nber.org/papers/w13868; Marjorie E. Wechsler, Kyra Caspary, Daniel C. Humphrey, and Kavita K. Matsko, "Examining the Effects of New Teacher Induction." Menlo Park, CA: SRI International, 2010.

14. Eric Isenberg, Steven Glazerman, Amy Johnson, Sarah Dolfin, and Martha Bleeker, "Linking Induction to Student Achievement." In *Past, Present, and Future Research on Teacher Induction,* edited by Jian Wang, Sandra J. Odell, and Renee T. Clift, 221–40. New York: Rowman & Littlefield Education, 2010.

15. Texas Center for Educational Research, "The Cost of Teacher Turnover." Austin, TX: Texas Center for Educational Research, October 2000. Accessed from: http://www.tasb.org/about/related/tcer/documents/17_teacher_turnover_full.pdf; Benjamin A. Cohen and Edward J. Fuller, "Effects of Mentoring and Induction on Beginning Teacher Retention." Paper presented at the Annual Meeting of the American Educational Research Association, San Francisco, California, April 2006.

16. Susan Moore Johnson, Susan M. Kardos, David Kauffman, Edward Liu, and Morgaen L. Donaldson. "The Support Gap: New Teachers' Early Experiences in High-Income and Low-Income Schools." *Education Policy Analysis Archives* 12 (2004): 61; Dan Lortie, *Schoolteacher: A Sociological Study.* London: University of Chicago Press, 1975.

17. Celine Coggins and Heather Peske, "New Teachers Are the New Majority." *Education Week,* January 18, 2011. Accessed from: www.edweek.org/ew/articles/2011/01/19/17coggins.h30.html.

18. Coggins and Peske, "New Teachers Are the New Majority."

19. MetLife, "The MetLife Survey of the American Teacher: Challenges for School Leadership." New York: Metropolitan Life Insurance Company, 2013. Accessed from: https://www.metlife.com/assets/cao/foundation/MetLife-Teacher -Survey-2012.pdf.

20. Sheryl Sandberg, *Lean In: Women, Work, and the Will to Lead.* New York: Random House, 2013.

# NEW TEACHER MENTORING PROGRAM
# ASSESSMENT RUBRIC

**I. FEATURES OF EFFECTIVE MENTORING PROGRAMS**
Successful mentoring programs carefully select, train, and utilize mentor's valuable skills and knowledge to support new teacher success.

| Emerging | Developing | Well Developed |
|---|---|---|
| **A. Careful Selection of Mentors** | | |
| The school/district has criteria for mentor selection, which may include knowledge of subject matter and students. | Program administrators develop a set of mentor selection criteria, which includes knowledge of subject matter and students. | Program leaders work with stakeholders to clearly define/articulate criteria for mentor selection, which include subject matter teaching and adult learning expertise. |
| Site administrators select and assign mentors as they see fit. | A mentor selection process is used to choose mentors from amongst volunteers. | A rigorous, transparent, and uniformly applied selection process is used to seek out, recruit, and choose highly skilled and knowledgeable teachers to become mentors. |
| **B. Increasing Mentor Capacity Through Rigorous Professional Development** | | |
| Mentor professional development occurs quarterly or less frequently. | Mentors participate in regular professional development. | Mentors participate in timely, regular, and ongoing professional development. |
| Mentor professional development includes mentoring language and skills. | Mentor professional development includes important topics such as adult learning theory, mentoring language and skills, and instructional coaching. | Mentors are provided with an intensive and structured curriculum of professional learning that is tailored to support mentor learning in key areas including adult learning theory, mentoring language and skills, and instructional coaching. |
| Mentors receive infrequent feedback from program leadership on their work with new teachers. | Mentors receive bi-annual or yearly feedback from program leadership or site administration on their work with new teachers. | Mentors set goals and develop individualize growth plans to meet those goals. Mentors receive regular feedback from program leaders to support their development. |
| **C. Strategic Deployment of Mentors** | | |
| New teachers are matched with mentors based on convenience for either the school or the mentor. | New teachers are often matched with mentors using a variety of criteria including content and grade level knowledge. | New teachers are consistently matched with mentors knowledgeable about how to teach their subject matter and/or grade level to all students. |
| | New teachers are often matched with mentors who have previously been successful teachers in the district. | New teachers are consistently matched with mentors knowledgeable about the school/context/students where the new teacher is working. |
| **D. Protected and Well-Used Mentoring Time** | | |
| Mentors and new teachers are expected to find time to meet outside school hours. | Time is provided for mentors and new teachers to meet at least weekly during the school day. | Protected time is provided for mentors and new teachers to regularly meet with and observe new teachers (1.5 hours per week/6-8 hours per month). |
| Mentors spend most of their time with new teachers focused on professional socialization and emotional support. | Mentors spend some of their time with new teachers engaged in mentoring processes that will improve instruction and student learning. | Mentors spend the majority of their time with new teachers engaged in rigorous mentoring processes that will improve immediate and long-term instruction and student learning. |
| New teachers are provided some mentoring for at least one year. | New teachers are provided some mentoring for at least two years. | New teachers are rigorously mentored for at least two years. |

| E. Using Data to Support Continuous Program Improvement | | |
|---|---|---|
| Program tracks basic data (i.e. numbers of new teachers and mentors, retention rates). | Program gathers implementation data (i.e. time spent with mentor, mentoring processes used, program quality). Some impact data on retention, teacher practice and student learning is also collected, perhaps anecdotally. | Program systematically gathers quantitative and qualitative implementation data (i.e. time spent with mentor, mentoring processes used, program quality) and seeks to show direct impact on retention, teacher practice and student learning. |
| Data mainly comes from mentoring program enrollment information (i.e. names of new teachers, pairings with mentors). | Data is mainly collected from mentors and new teachers. Data from other sources is not gathered regularly or systematically. | Data is collected from multiple sources including mentors, new teachers, principals, students, and other stakeholders. |

| II. TAILORING MENTORING SUPPORT | | |
|---|---|---|
| Successful mentoring programs tailor support to match the diverse needs and strengths of new teachers. | | |
| Emerging | Developing | Well Developed |
| A. Consideration of New Teacher Needs and Experiences | | |
| Mentors may ask questions about teachers' background and learning styles in order to build a trusting relationship with the new teacher. | Mentors are asked to learn about new teachers as people and as professionals in order to build a relationship and make decisions about how best to work with new teachers. | Mentors gather data about teachers' preparation, perceptions of readiness, educational philosophy, prior work experiences, personal experiences and preferences to plan appropriately tailored induction experiences. |
| B. Planning for New Teacher Growth and Development | | |
| Mentors explain professional teaching standards and processes for mentoring work to new teachers. | Mentors gather data and make assessments of the strengths and needs of new teachers against professional teaching standards.<br><br>Mentors make decisions about what new teachers need in order to grow. | Mentors and new teachers regularly work together to co-assess new teachers' strengths and needs against a set of professional teaching standards and to set meaningful goals aligned with new teacher needs and interests.<br><br>Mentors and new teachers plan a rigorous course of work that supports new teachers in making progress towards those goals. |
| C. Tailoring Mentoring Programs to Appropriately Support New Teacher Needs | | |
| Mentors work through a proscribed mentoring curriculum with new teachers. | Mentors use a mentoring curriculum system that provides some options related to processes for the mentor.<br><br>Some differentiated options are available for new teachers, especially for Special Educators, those who already hold a credential, and other special cases. | Mentors understand their role is to tailor mentoring to best fit each new teacher's assessed needs and context in order to ensure the rapid growth and development of each new teacher.<br><br>Mentors know how to use a set of flexible processes to guide their interactions with new teachers, gather data on classroom practice and student learning, foster reflection, and provide accountability. |

## III. ADMINISTRATIVE SUPPORT AND SCHOOL CONTEXT

**Successful mentoring programs work in coordination with school-based leaders to create a working environment conducive to new teacher success.**

| Emerging | Developing | Well Developed |
|---|---|---|
| **A. Sustainably Assigning New Teachers** | | |
| Site administrators place new teachers in open positions.<br><br>New teachers must create and/or find materials resources necessary to teach their classes. | Site administrators work to create teaching assignments that attempt to minimize extra duties or multiple preps.<br><br>New teachers are provided some basic materials necessary to teach their classes. | Site administrators create teaching assignments with reasonable workloads for new teachers that are appropriate for their level of experience (i.e. not given the most challenging classes, multiple preps, or roving assignments).<br><br>New teachers are provided with the resources and materials necessary to effectively teach their assigned classes. |
| **B. Providing Opportunities for Planning and Collaboration with Colleagues** | | |
| New teachers are provided with regularly scheduled planning time.<br><br>Time with colleagues occurs primarily during grade- or department-level meetings.<br><br>New teachers sometimes attend professional learning events outside their school related to department, school, or district priorities. | New teachers are provided with planning/collaboration time with other teachers in their grade/subject monthly or bi-monthly.<br><br>Time with colleagues is in professional learning communities that may focus on student data.<br><br>New teachers may attend other professional learning events outside their school that will support their ongoing learning. | New teachers are provided with regularly scheduled planning/collaboration time with other teachers in the same grade/subject weekly or bi-weekly.<br><br>Time with colleagues is spent in ongoing and collaborative inquiry that leads to instructional improvement and student learning.<br><br>New teachers are purposefully connected with a professional learning community that extends beyond their grade level, school, or district that supports teachers' individualized needs for ongoing professional learning. |
| **C. Deepening Mentor-Administrator Connections** | | |
| Site administrators and mentors do not meet unless there is an issue of concern that needs to be addressed. | Mentors or site administrators may call meetings when needed to discuss issues related to new teacher development, issues of concern, alignment of support, or to discuss growth at end of the year. | Mentors, program leaders, and site-based administrators meet regularly to learn about and discuss issues related to new teacher development, school goals, and integration of new teacher support into school systems and structures. |
| **D. Fostering Positive New Teacher-Administrator Relationships** | | |
| Site administrators observe new teachers the required number of times during the year and meet to discuss progress and contract renewal. | Site administrators observe new teachers periodically throughout the year and provide feedback related to school goals. Some observations may be formative in nature. | Site administrators work to develop relationships with new teachers early in the year, help them set appropriate goals, observe teachers regularly in a formative capacity, and provide timely, positive, and useful feedback related to their progress towards those goals. |

# Section I: Features
# of Effective Mentoring

This section explores how to make the most of mentors. Readers will consider: strategies for identifying and recruiting high-quality mentor candidates; ideas for creating highly effective mentors through the development of a rigorous professional learning program; how to strategically deploy mentors to make the best use of their knowledge and skills; and strategies to make the best use of mentoring time. Program leaders will consider what is known about each of these areas, consider their own programs' strengths and areas for growth, and set next steps for success.

Effective mentors are at the heart of every high-quality induction program. A growing body of research indicates that a quality, highly trained, and supported mentor can accelerate the development of classroom teachers and improve student learning. Therefore, the selection, training, ongoing support, and thoughtful use of teacher mentors is critical to providing instructionally focused support to beginning teachers.

In the recruitment and selection process, leaders must keep in mind that not all good teachers make good mentors. The skills and abilities of an effective mentor are different from those of an effective classroom teacher. These skills include facilitating adult learning, collecting relevant classroom observation data, providing effective feedback, leading reflective conversations, and using grade-level or content-specific coaching skills. Foundational mentor training and ongoing professional development are important tools to ensure mentors develop these skills and effectively make the transition from classroom teacher to mentor. Being a good teacher alone does not prepare mentors to work with teachers in a wide range of subjects, grade levels, and contexts. Being an excellent third-grade teacher, even when that teacher receives basic mentor training, does not necessarily make her able to effectively support a high school

Algebra teacher. Pairing mentors with beginning teachers of similar teaching and/or school assignments is another important consideration when developing a mentoring program.

Mentors also need time to do their jobs well. When mentors do not have release time to work in the classrooms of new teachers, a lot can get missed. They may miss the small, remarkable observations that can change a teacher's life: the inefficient way students pass in papers, the slow pacing of lesson that leads to student behavioral issues, the example that helped to clarify a challenging concept for students. Short of restructuring the school day to increase professional learning time for all teachers, employing full-time mentors and providing regular release from classroom teaching duties are effective strategies to provide mentors and new teachers with dedicated time to excel in their roles. Even when school districts do create full-time mentoring positions, program leaders still need to be mindful about time. Program leaders need to consider the number of new teachers a mentor can reasonably and effectively support in conjunction with the other aspects of their job (i.e., planning, professional learning, other assigned duties). It would be mistake, for example, to assigned a full-time mentor to work with thirty new teachers. There are simply not enough hours in the day or week for a mentor to meet with each of those new teachers on her caseload, let alone to meaningfully support each one. This is particularly compounded if those new teachers are spread out over a variety of school sites, meaning that the mentor must spend time driving between sites and coordinating between various bell schedules.

So how can schools/districts ensure they choose the best mentors, provide them with the training they need, and use their skills in the best possible way? In order to answer that question, this chapter explores four features of how to best use expert classroom teachers who have stepped into a mentoring role as they work to meet the complex needs of new teachers. These four features include:

- careful selection of mentors
- increased mentor capacity through rigorous professional development
- strategic deployment of mentors
- protected and well-used mentoring time

This chapter will provide key ideas in each of these areas, and it will support program leaders in considering their strengths and areas for growth related to the selection and development of mentor teachers.

# 1

# Careful Selection of Mentors

**Well Developed**

*Program leaders work with stakeholders to clearly define/articulate criteria for mentor selection, which include subject matter teaching and adult learning expertise.*

*A rigorous, transparent, and uniformly applied selection process is used to seek out, recruit, and choose highly skilled and knowledgeable teachers to become mentors.*

Mentoring programs rise and fall on the success of their mentors because, potentially, mentors assume a significant and powerful role in their schools and districts. Through their role, mentors become on-the-job teacher educators who very directly influence the professional norms and teaching practices of new teachers who, in turn, will be educating the next generation of students in our schools. Thus, it is crucial for program leaders to be very clear about exactly what the norms and instructional practices they want to establish in schools and classrooms are and to be very selective in choosing mentors who can support the implementation of that vision.

Mentor teachers, if carefully selected, can help create new norms of collaboration, inquiry, and ongoing learning that can spread across an entire school or district. The positive, empowered, professional model effective mentors present to new teachers conveys the high standards of performance expected by the school and profession as a whole. In addition to bringing deep expertise in their own grade level or subject matter, mentors can reinforce positive attitudes and beliefs about students and the role of the teacher in students' academic lives. They can model a dedication to professional growth by being constantly curious about their practice and student work, constantly seeking to improve, working with others to learn, and holding themselves personally accountable for their own growth as well as the academic success of all their students. These are the mentors who will make a difference in the lives of new teachers and students.

Mentors also have an important role beyond working one-to-one with novice teachers as models of professional leadership and ambassadors for the mentoring program of which they are a part. As part of their work, mentors seek to establish positive, collaborative, and successful relationships with site administrators, other teachers, parents, union leaders, and university faculty. Their reputation as highly effective educators as well as their professional poise, sense of purpose, and effective communication skills bring credibility to the induction program, its work, and its leadership.

One of the first things a school or district needs to consider when reviewing its mentoring program is to ensure that the right people are becoming mentors. Consider the following questions:

1. What selection criteria are used to locate potential mentors?
2. What process is used to locate potential mentors?
3. How are mentors selected?
4. How long will mentors serve, and what will be their career path after serving as a mentor?

The answers to each of these questions greatly impact the process of ensuring that the people most likely to be effective mentors, who can quickly move new teachers and their students, are identified and chosen for this important job. In the following section, we will explore each of these areas and consider ways these questions can impact the success of an induction program.

## SELECTION CRITERIA

The recruitment and selection of mentors is arguably the single most important task facing a mentoring program's leadership. Therefore, thoughtfully considering the criteria for their selection is a first priority. While specific mentoring and coaching skills can be learned through intensive and ongoing mentor professional development, there are some important attributes, experiences, and traits that potential mentors should possess.

In a quick review of the thirty-one states that currently have induction policies and standards in place, there appears to be a wide array of selection criteria that range from broad and vague to very specific. Here are a few highlights:

- California Induction Program Standards require the assignment of mentors "using well-defined criteria consistent with the provider's assigned responsibilities in the program."
- Connecticut requires mentor teachers to demonstrate: (1) effective teaching practice; (2) the ability to work cooperatively as a team member to aid the professional growth of a beginning teacher; (3) professional commitment to improving the induction of beginning teachers; (4) the ability to relate effectively to adult learners; and (5) the ability to be reflective and articulate about the craft of teaching.
- New Jersey state law establishes minimum criteria for mentor selection. Criteria include: (1) a minimum of three years of experience in the district; (2) teacher commitment to the goals of the local mentor plan; (3) confidentiality with the new teacher; (4) demonstrated exemplary command of content-area knowledge and of pedagogy; (5) experience and certification in the subject area in which the novice teacher is teaching; (6) knowledge about the social and workplace norms; (7) knowledge about the resources and opportunities in the district; (8) letters of recommendation; and (9) agreement to complete comprehensive mentor training.
- South Carolina requires each district to evaluate the performance of each mentor teacher on: (1) knowledge of beginning-teacher professional development and effective adult learning strategies; (2) familiarity with the state's performance assessment system; (3) knowledge of researched-based instructional strategies and effective student assessment; (4) understanding of the importance of an educator having a thorough command of the subject matter and teaching skills; (5) understanding of the importance of literacy in the classroom; (6) the record of exemplary teaching and professional conduct; (7) effective interpersonal and communication skills; (8) demonstrated commitment to his or her own professional growth and learning; (9) the willingness and the ability to participate in professional preparation to acquire the knowledge and skills needed to be an effective mentor; (10) the willingness and ability to engage in nonevaluative assessment processes, including the ability to hold planning and reflective conversations with beginning teachers about their classroom practice; (11) the willingness and ability to work collaboratively and share instructional ideas and materials with beginning teachers; and (12) the willingness and ability to deepen his or her understanding of cultural, racial, ethnic, linguistic, and cognitive diversity.[1]

Looking across these and a number of other state and local induction program guidelines, it appears that many mentors are chosen initially because they have a reputation as effective classroom teachers. This is not unusual. In gathering data about a wide variety of induction programs in the United States, a track record of successful teaching experience is the most common characteristic listed in the job description of mentors. Some additional common characteristics of and criteria for selecting mentor teachers are: a clearly articulated vision of teaching and learning, knowledge of content, accomplished curriculum developer, professional interests, expressed educational philosophies, and compatible personalities.[2]

It seems reasonable at first glance that the most common criteria for selecting mentor teachers are their skills as a classroom educator. Given that mentors will be role models for new teachers, we want our new teachers to be mentored by those who are passionate about their profession, their students, and their content, and who have had great success.

However, being a good teacher of students does not automatically mean that one will be a successful mentor of adults because providing professional development for teachers requires an entirely different skill set than teaching students. Not only must the mentor understand the content and how to teach it to students in a deep way, they must also know how to connect and build trust with another adult, assess the strengths and needs of a teacher, work collaboratively, be flexible, be responsible for maintaining records, not to mention want to learn how to do all of this!

Below is a list of mentor selection criteria that may be used as a good jumping-off point for many schools and districts:

### SAMPLE MENTOR SELECTION CRITERIA

Mentor selection criteria include, but are not limited to, the following:

1. Recognition as an exemplary classroom teacher and excellent professional role model.
2. Current or former classroom teacher with a record of at least three years successful teaching experience with a wide range of students.
3. Strong subject matter and/or grade-level appropriate knowledge.
4. Effective interpersonal and communication skills.
5. Credibility with peers and administrators.
6. Respect for multiple perspectives.
7. Experience working effectively with linguistically and culturally diverse students and special populations.
8. Understands the value of confidentiality in the mentoring process and is able to maintain confidentiality in mentoring relationships.
9. Demonstrated commitment to personal and professional growth and learning.
10. Willingness to participate in professional preparation to acquire the knowledge and skills needed to be an effective mentor.
11. Willingness to work collaboratively with beginning teachers, mentors, and program leadership.
12. Knowledge of/willingness to learn about adult learning theory and beginning teacher development.
13. Commitment to improving the academic lives of all students.

This set of criteria do include being an exemplary teacher, and also to recognize the other skills that mentors need to have in order to be successful in working effectively with adults, learning the new skill set associated with mentoring, and sharing content- or grade-specific instructional skills.

As you consider the needs of your school, district, or program, you will want to tailor your list to include the criteria that mentors will need to be highly effective in your unique context. For example, is your school or district in an urban context? Would an understanding of that context and the unique needs of students and teachers within that context be an asset for a mentor? Are there a large number of English learners? Or is there an initiative in your district that mentoring could support? Currently, some programs are using their mentors to support new teachers in implementing the Common Core, address technology integration, and to support dialogue about equity and bias in the classroom, all of which are thoughtful decisions made by program leaders to align mentoring support with the needs and goals of the school or district.

Whatever the criteria for selecting mentors you decide is appropriate for your context, it is important to make sure these requirements are clearly defined and represent a shared understanding among stakeholders and potential mentors. In many programs, leaders reach out to groups who might be involved with mentoring or the results of mentoring, such as: current mentors, site and district administrators, curriculum developers, human resources, teachers, association leaders, and university representatives to help in the development of these criteria. As you think about the stakeholders in your program, consider who is currently involved in the development of such criteria, as well as who else could provide useful insight in this process.

## FINDING POTENTIAL MENTORS

Once you've got a clearly defined set of selection criteria, it's time to find potential mentors. Strategies for recruiting mentors range from opportunistic appointment to promoting self-nomination to tying mentoring to a developmental career ladder. The problem with these approaches is that they rely on people self-selecting into the program for a wide variety of reasons or being chosen for arbitrary reasons. They do not necessarily lead to getting the right people in the door of your program.

During the initial stages of developing an induction program, or when a program is undergoing an overhaul, it is imperative that the mentor selection process includes an aggressive recruitment effort. Many schools and districts may lack the structures to assess who their most skilled educators are, or which of their teachers are having a strong, positive impact on student outcomes.

Even when excellent veteran teachers can be identified, they are often reluctant to leave their classrooms either part or full time or to take on additional responsibilities while maintaining a full teaching load, especially to step into a role that has not existed before or into one that has not been held in high status in the past. Interestingly, it is often the exemplary veteran teachers whose commitment to their students and to their practice that make the most ideal mentor candidates and who are most reluctant to step out of their classrooms for any part of the day or for an extended period of time. However, as previously mentioned, not all excellent teachers make good support providers for beginning teachers, so even those identified as high quality may not be the right fit.

The selection process is further complicated by the fact that school administrators are sometimes more than a little bit hesitant to recommend their best teachers for other roles that might lead to teachers leaving their classroom all together. This is reasonable given that the goal of site administrators is to find and retain the best possible teachers to work with the students in that building.

What this means for induction program leaders is that simply posting the job of mentor and listing the qualifications may not be enough to get the right people in the door. Instead, program leaders need to educate those who may be hesitant about the long-term gains as well as the large-scale impacts that mentoring can have. They also need to help create the systems that can identify top-performing educators who meet their criteria. Then, program leaders, site administrators, stakeholders, and other mentors can work together to actively search for and contact strong classroom teachers with the qualities they know will lead to successful mentoring in order to build a robust pool of candidates from which to choose.

Some districts are addressing the challenge of finding the right people to mentor by recruiting and training more mentors each year than are actually selected to serve in that capacity. For example, in one Florida district, a large pool of mentors is selected and receives training together. Some are currently mentoring, while the rest, which they refer to as "Mentors in Waiting," remain in their classrooms but are already fully trained and ready to begin serving as mentors as soon as there is a need. Given that this district puts a term limit of three years on mentor service, having a fully trained and ready pool of replacements to fill the slots of those stepping down each year eases the transition period and learning curve that learning to mentor can entail. It also means that there are more teachers in each school who are learning the valuable mentoring practices and teacher leadership skills that mentors gain and can spread those practices across schools and districts at a much more rapid pace.[3]

Similarly, an Arizona district has solved the problem of finding mentors by maintaining a cadre of carefully trained master teachers known as

Instructional Program Specialists. These are classroom teachers employed on teacher contracts but deployed on "special assignment," a significant portion of which is to support new teachers through a three-year formal mentoring relationship. These specialists receive ongoing training in coaching and curriculum and work directly with new teachers in their classrooms as well as with other veteran teachers.[4]

A number of other districts across the country are also finding that combining instructional coaching and mentoring roles into singular jobs makes a great deal of sense in terms of finances (singular positions instead of many part-time people), as well as in terms of consolidating training and support for coaches, aligning and implementing grade or content initiatives across all teachers both new and veteran with whom the coach works, and ensuring that there are people with content, grade-level, or special expertise (e.g., special education) on tap to mentor when needed.

Another option is to use retired teachers as mentors. In a number of districts throughout the county, schools and districts are finding that they have a pool of excellent veteran teachers who are no longer teaching but who are interested in continuing to be involved in education in a part-time capacity to maintain their health benefits, or to earn some additional income, or just to stay close to the students and schools they love. There are many advantages to using retired teachers as mentors. They know the school or district well, are knowledgeable about their grade and subject area, have time to commit to mentoring, and do not require pulling a current classroom teacher away from students, which can be highly attractive to many districts.

It is important to take a pause here for a minute and talk about a few ways that are not as effective in selecting mentors, but which at first glance may seem appealing to some programs. Particularly in small schools or districts, or when funds are not readily available, it is easy to be drawn toward selecting people who may not be the best choice in the long run. Here are a few examples:

1. *Using school administrators as mentors.* While it may seem like a great idea at first glance to use site or district administrators as mentors because there is a desire to create a closer school community where teachers and administrators have a close working relationship, or they are already freed from classroom duties, or because it is important for administrators to have many of the same skills as mentors in supporting and developing teachers, or because it seems cost effective to do so, there are a number of problems with this idea.

   It is important to understand that a mentor's job is to be a confidential *formative* assessor and instructional coach for a new teacher. The new teacher must feel free to say anything he or she is feeling or thinking, must be willing to take risks instructionally in front of the mentor, must be willing to ask for help, and must know that what the mentor and the new teacher do together will not, in any way, be shared with others without the consent of the new teacher.

A critical role of administrators—to *summatively* assess teacher performance and make decisions about teacher employment—does not mesh well with the mentoring role. It is too hard for both the administrator/mentor and the new teacher to know when the mentor/administrator is wearing the mentoring hat and when he/she is wearing the administrator hat. It is impossible to fully separate the two roles and will always result in a new teacher not taking the risks necessary to grow, holding back their words, curtailing their actions, and not growing to their full potential.

Additionally, one of the biggest frustrations heard from those who have tried to wear both the administrative and mentor hats is not having enough time to mentor well. Mentoring requires meeting with the new teacher on a regular basis (The New Teacher Center recommends an average of 1.5 hours per week), and most administrators cannot plan for that kind of regular time because as all administrators know, your schedule is not fully under your control. Administrator/ mentors often must cancel meetings with new teachers to deal with pressing school issues, leaving large gaps in time between mentor meetings and lost opportunities for learning and teacher growth.

Generally, programs that attempt to use this administrator/mentor model eventually separate the mentoring and administrative roles in order to salvage their mentoring programs.

2. *Using nonreleased classroom teachers as mentors.* Some schools opt to use teachers with no release time for mentoring to work with a small handful of new teachers. The belief is that, for a small stipend, they will be able to find time during planning periods and before or after school to work with new teachers, and that this is sufficient time for mentoring.

While this may seem like a reasonable solution, particularly when resources are tight, this is not a good option. Most often, those who are selected to be mentors in this kind of system are that handful of teacher leaders in a school who already have a large number of responsibilities beyond teaching, such as coaching a sport, sponsoring a club, serving on the school leadership team, acting as department chair, not to mention family and community commitments.

To truly be effective, the mentor must be able to spend time in the new teacher's classroom, observing and gathering data, coteaching or modeling lessons, and supporting the teacher in working with students. They also need to be able to attend training with other mentors to learn and grow the skills necessary to do their jobs well.

When mentors and new teachers can only meet outside of teaching hours, the mentor's other commitments often take precedence over meeting with new teachers. Meetings set during lunch and common planning times do not allow mentors to do the kind of observational in-classroom work that is central to mentoring. And, with all of their free time taken up with mentoring or other activities, when will they find time for growing their mentoring skills?

This option generally leads to "buddy mentoring," wherein the teacher gets someone to talk to and to offer them copies of lesson plans or resources but does not get "instructional mentoring" that leads to a growth of teacher awareness, knowledge, and skill under the close guidance of a knowledgeable veteran mentor. As Paul Lehman notes, "The multi-year induction program that provides systematic help and support cannot be adequately done by another teacher with a full-time load who drops by when time permits or when a problem arises."[5] This option is little better than having no program at all.

Using full-time mentors, released from all classroom-teaching duties, provides for the greatest amount of flexibility to meet with, observe, and provide feedback to beginning teachers. It allows mentors to focus exclusively on their critical role in supporting beginning educators. In addition to freeing mentor teachers from balancing mentoring duties with a full (or reduced) teaching load, employing fewer full-time mentors allows induction programs to be more selective and choose the highest-quality candidates for this important role.

## WHEN FULL-TIME MENTORS JUST AREN'T AN OPTION

In an ideal situation, mentors would be released from their classrooms so that their full-time job is supporting new teachers. However, for many schools and districts, this full-release model just isn't an option. Perhaps there are not enough new teachers in a school or district to warrant a full-time mentor, or perhaps fully releasing a teacher is cost prohibitive. Many successful mentoring programs facing these challenges choose to use partially released mentors with great success. In this partial-release model, mentors either teach part of the day or they are assigned to other tasks such as instructional coaching to round out their workload.

Mentors who are assigned to teach part of the day often have the most challenging of these two scenarios. There is no substantial research on how to appropriately balance mentoring and teaching. However, anecdotally, we know that trying to teach and mentor is a delicate balancing act. For anyone who has ever tried to hold two or more professional roles simultaneously, you know how hard it is to keep either one within the stated percentage. Inevitably, it feels like you are working two full-time jobs instead of two 50 percent time jobs, for example.

For programs that are considering releasing mentors part time from their teaching positions, it is important to consider how much time mentors truly need to do that job well as well as the logistics of when mentoring interactions with new teachers as well as professional learning experiences need to take place. For example, mentors need to spend time meeting to lesson plan and problem solve with new teachers regularly, which is an activity that can take place at a scheduled time every week. That is reasonably easy to schedule. Mentors also need time in new teachers' classrooms observing to gather data and to provide specific feedback on teaching and learning. This is harder to schedule consistently, as it is often based on when in the day the new teacher is teaching that topic or needs support to problem solve a management issue. When mentors are tied to classrooms for some part of the day, they cannot as easily schedule observations to best meet the needs of new teachers. In addition, mentors need time to plan for their interactions with new teachers, to complete documentation, and to gather resources. This preparation and follow-up time is often not considered when setting up mentor-teaching positions and can be very time consuming. When mentors are also responsible for preparing lessons for their own students as well as grading papers, attending meetings, and collaborating with parents, the important work of planning for work with new teachers can fall by the wayside.

There is no perfect ratio of teaching load to mentoring load, as it is dependent on a wide variety of factors such as those described above. If a school or district chooses this option, it is simply important to remember these variables and weigh the possibilities carefully in order to create a schedule that meets the needs of the mentor/teacher, the new teacher, and the students involved.

Combining mentoring duties with other nonclassroom roles such as content or instructional coaches is a trend that seems to be on the rise. Many programs and districts look at the knowledge and skills necessary to be an effective mentor and see an immediate application to other coaching roles. There is, in fact, so much commonality between these roles that in some programs such as the TriValley Teacher Induction Program in California, mentors and instructional coaches regularly attend joint professional development even when mentors and instructional coaches are not in blended roles. It becomes logical, therefore, that when fully releasing a mentor is not an option, these two similar roles should be paired together when possible.[6]

Unlike those serving in mentor-teacher roles, mentor-instructional coaches have the benefit of being released from their classrooms, allowing them to visit and observe on a more flexible basis. However, as mentioned above, holding multiple roles means having to deal with logistical challenges as well as the difficulty of trying to keep each part of your role within its appropriate percentage.

When considering possible mentor candidates whether for full-release, partial-release, or blended positions, the best option is to find current or recent teachers or instructional coaches who have dedicated time during their day to work with new teachers and who have the time and interest to learn the skills necessary to be an effective mentor. This might be current classroom teachers with dedicated release time for mentoring and training, it might be instructional coaches whose full-time job is working with teachers and whose skills would be enhanced through learning to mentor, or it may be retired teachers. Those with roles that require them to evaluate teachers or make decisions about employment and those with no time to learn the necessary skills to mentor well or who have no time to do the observational work that is at the heart of mentoring are not good choices.

Whether you decide to recruit only enough mentors to fill current vacancies, recruit a larger pool of potential mentors, or are considering consolidating mentoring and instructional coaching positions, The New Teacher Center suggests the following recruitment strategies to help get the right people into the hiring pool:

## NEW MENTOR RECRUITMENT TIPS

- **Keep Your Eyes and Ears Open**
  Once program leaders are clear on the selection criteria and the qualities they are looking for in good mentors, informal observation and discussion can take place. Having conversations with principals and other teachers, mentors, or coaches can often lead to identifying possible mentors. A personal approach with a suggestion encouraging a teacher to apply for the position could follow. Care needs to be taken to explain that there is an open and rigorous selection process, conducted by a representative committee, and that the invitation to apply is the first in a sequence of events and will not necessarily lead to a job offer.

- **So You Want to Be a Mentor**
  Some districts hold an information session, open house, or reception, inviting teachers who may be interested in being a mentor. Program information can be shared and mentors and beginning teachers can provide "testimonials" about their collaborative work.

- **A Day in the Life of a Mentor**
  A meeting or workshop showing "a day in the life of a mentor" is another way of providing a detailed description of the roles and responsibilities of the mentor. This works well with a media presentation and a follow-up question and answer period.

- **Event Participation**
  Inviting potential candidates to a mentor training, a beginning teacher workshop facilitated by the mentors, or a mentor meeting is another way for teachers to consider mentoring possibilities. Or a candidate could shadow another mentor during an observation or conversation with a beginning teacher.

(*Source*: New Teacher Center, 2011.)

As schools and districts consider their unique context, it is important to think about the processes and venues through which they might be able to find out more about who the highly effective teachers are that might also be great mentors. How might a school or district find the right people to mentor? In working through this process, remember that the work of hiring the highest-caliber mentors is important and will have a direct impact on student-learning gains.

## THE SELECTION PROCESS

So now you have done the hard work of aggressively recruiting exceptional teachers to create a pool of mentor candidates from whom to choose. How do you go about selecting the right ones?

Remember, like the process of developing mentor criteria, the selection process should also be as inclusive as possible. This means that other stakeholders such as site administrators, union leaders, veteran teacher leaders, and others should be involved.

While having a variety of stakeholders present on the selection committee ensures that all parties have a voice and a stake in making the program a success, their participation in the selection process makes it incumbent upon the program leaders to ensure that the interview panel has a common vision of what a "quality mentor" is, and that everyone understands and accepts the selection criteria. As you convene your hiring committee, make sure that the selection criteria, along with the roles and responsibilities associated with the position, are clearly conveyed.

Once all members of the committee are clear about the criteria, it's time to consider the process of selection. Induction programs use a wide range of processes to learn about the potential of mentor candidates. Among the most common are:

- written response to questions (scenarios, philosophy of teaching, why the candidate is interested in mentoring, etc.)
- classroom observation of the candidate while he/she is teaching
- panel interview, often consisting of responses to mentoring scenarios

Much like hiring teachers, it is very difficult to judge a candidates' practice by their words in an interview. So while these are all useful and beneficial ways of finding information about potential candidates, they don't show a panel what the candidate can do in an actual mentoring situation.

One possibility is to simulate a mentoring situation for the candidate through the use of video. In one California program, induction leaders show mentor candidates a video of a new teacher teaching and then ask the mentor to describe how he or she might support this new teacher.

What the mentors notice (or do not notice), what they choose to focus on, the language they use to describe the situation, and the attitude with which they approach the exercise can reveal a great deal about the potential candidate.

As you consider the process you use to select candidates, consider how you are gathering accurate data about how a potential mentor might actually work in his or her role. What kinds of experiences might you create that would support you in making the best decision possible about whom to select?

## BUILDING A CAREER PATHWAY FOR MENTORS

As program leaders go through the process of recruiting and selecting mentors, candidates will most likely have some important career-related questions as they decide whether to apply for these positions, such as:

- Is there a minimum amount of time or a time limit on how long I can mentor?
- What are my options after I mentor? Am I guaranteed my teaching position back? Will my mentoring experience qualify me for other leadership roles in my school or district?

Every school and district answers these questions differently depending on context, need, and other contractual factors. However, they are important for program leaders to have considered as they develop their program.

Some schools and districts create specific parameters around how long mentors can serve, while others do not. For example, some districts specify that mentors may only mentor for three years because they want the leadership knowledge and skills mentors gain from the experience to be spread across a wider cross section of the teaching population. The time limit ensures more teachers get the experience of mentoring and more people with current or prior mentoring experience are currently in schools. Other programs intentionally do not put time limits on mentoring. They trade a wider cross section of teachers with mentoring skills for a small group who, with prolonged practice and support, develop deeper skill sets and may be able to hone their skills and move new teachers more quickly as a result. Whether your program decides to set time limits on mentor service or not, it is important to make these decisions prior to recruiting potential mentors.

Connected to time limits is the question of what mentors can do after they complete their mentoring service. For example, are mentors guaranteed a teaching position in their home school or district afterward? Are there any union rules that should be considered in this decision? Perhaps there are other roles mentors might be eligible for as a result of the mentoring experiences. Many mentors go on to become school or district administrators or serve in other leadership positions. Having former mentors as principals spreads the knowledge of the value of mentoring programs to other parts of the school system, which is, of course, quite valuable for program leaders. Whatever the possible career paths mentors might be able to take after they serve as mentors, having an answer for this question is important as program leaders go through the mentor recruitment and selection process.

## MAKING MENTORING WORK FOR YOU

Choosing the right people to become mentors can make or break an induction program. Therefore, it is imperative that those tasked with beginning or overhauling a mentoring program:

1. work with stakeholders to clearly define the criteria for potential mentors that include both teaching expertise as well as skills in working with adult learners
2. seek out potentially effective mentors through a wide array of recruitment strategies, including classroom observations, partnerships with other stakeholders familiar with your criteria, and through education of the community about the mentoring position
3. consider whether your school or district needs and can afford full-release mentors. If the answer is no, consider other possible alternatives to combine positions that provide as much release time and similar job responsibilities as possible
4. use a rigorous process to select mentors that involves input from multiple stakeholders
5. consider whether there will be term limits for mentors and the positives and drawbacks of this decision for mentors, new teachers, and the school or district
6. explore possible career options for mentors after their mentor service

A close look at these processes can provide a strong beginning to any program. However, simply finding the right people to serve as mentors is not enough. New mentors also need structured support to learn about their new role and grow in this new position.

## READY TO TAKE THE NEXT STEP?

At the end of this section, there is a Discussion Guide designed to help program leaders consider the key ideas discussed in this chapter. These questions are designed to support you in beginning the important discussions about these key topics with other stakeholders and decision makers in your organization.

## NOTES

1. New Teacher Center,"State Policy Reviews." Santa Cruz, CA: Author, 2014. Accessed from: http://www.newteachercenter.org/policy/policy-map.

2. Sharon Feiman-Nemser, "Teacher Mentoring: A Critical Review." *ERIC Digest* 95, no. 2 (July 1996). Accessed from: http://eric.ed.gov/?id=ED397060; B. A. Tillman, "Quiet Leadership: Informal Mentoring of Beginning Teachers." *Momentum* 31, no. 1 (2000): 24–26.

3. Susan Villani, *Comprehensive Mentoring Programs for New Teachers: Models of Induction and Support*. San Francisco: Corwin Press, 2002.

4. Ibid.

5. Paul R. Lehman, "Ten Steps to School Reform at Bargain Prices." *Education Week* 23, no. 13 (November 26, 2003): 36, 28.

6. Kim Ortiz (TriValley Teacher Induction Project director) in discussion with the author, November 2013.

# 2

# ✛

# Increasing Mentor Capacity through Rigorous Professional Development

| Well Developed |
|---|
| *Mentors participate in timely, regular, and ongoing professional development.* |
| *Mentors are provided with an intensive and structured curriculum of professional learning that is tailored to support mentor learning in key areas including adult learning theory, mentoring language and skills, and instructional coaching.* |
| *Mentors set goals and develop individualize growth plans to meet those goals. Mentors receive regular feedback from program leaders to support their development.* |

Once you have selected the best possible veteran teachers to serve as mentors, it is time to consider the way in which you will support them in making the transition to this new role so they can continue to grow as educators, teacher leaders, and mentors. Just as the quality of instruction that students receive has a tremendous impact on their performance, the quality of mentoring that new teachers receive can significantly influence their development. Therefore, it is imperative that mentoring programs carefully consider how they provide mentors with the knowledge and skills they need to provide new teachers with a quality induction experience capable of quickly growing teacher practice.

Effective professional development enables mentors to develop the knowledge and skills they need to address both the needs of the new teacher as well as the learning needs of students. To be effective, professional development requires thoughtful planning followed by careful implementation with feedback to ensure it is responding appropriately to mentors' learning needs. Mentors must then put their new knowledge and skills to work. Professional development is not effective unless it causes mentors to improve their ability to accelerate the instructional growth of the teachers they support. The effectiveness of professional development truly depends on how carefully educators conceive, plan, and implement it.[1]

Research shows that there are some key components of effective professional development for teachers that are just as relevant when applied to mentors.

Effective professional development:

- is ongoing
- includes training, practice, and feedback; opportunities for individual reflection and group inquiry into practice; and coaching or other follow-up procedures
- is embedded in teacher/mentor work
- is collaborative, providing opportunities for teachers to interact with peers
- focuses on student/new teacher/mentor learning, which should, in part, guide assessment of its effectiveness
- encourages and supports school-based and teacher initiatives
- is rooted in the knowledge base for teaching
- incorporates constructivist approaches to teaching and learning
- recognizes teachers/mentors as professionals and adult learners
- provides adequate time and follow-up support[2]

Given these broad parameters, there are many ways to go about organizing a mentoring program, and no one way works best. Therefore, this section will only speak generally about areas that mentoring programs should consider as they organize their programs, not about the specifics of organizing content for learning. However, having a broad, general understanding and a foundation from which to build upon is a vital first step in tailoring your professional development to the unique needs of your organization. Leaders can ask themselves:

1. How much time do mentors have to attend professional development? At the beginning of the year for initial training? Across the year?
2. Are the topics discussed during mentor professional development sufficient to support mentor practice and teacher growth? Do they support continued mentor development over time?
3. How are mentors supported in meaningfully developing their own skills as individual educators, teacher leaders, and mentors by program leadership?

Organizing effective professional development for mentors is not an easy task. This section will explore each of these areas in depth and consider how programs might deepen their own structures to further the development of their mentors.

## TIME: PROVIDING REGULAR PROFESSIONAL DEVELOPMENT ACROSS THE YEAR

As with all things in education, finding the time to provide professional development for mentors is a challenge for induction program leaders. Mentoring requires a complex skill set that is different from the one required to teach students and, therefore, requires time to learn deeply and well so they can use their skills effectively with new teachers. When done well, professional development can support mentors in developing as a community, learn and deepen their understanding of the requisite skills and knowledge needed to do their jobs effectively, and provide them with opportunities to practice and gain confidence in new skills before going out into the field on their own.

As discussed in the broad outlines of effective professional development research described above, mentors, like teachers, need time. Time to understand new concepts; learn new skills; and develop new attitudes through research, assessment, discussion, and reflection. They need time to try new approaches and integrate them into their practice. They also need time to plan their own professional development.[3] Joseph Cambone further points out that mentors and teachers, as adult learners, need both set-aside time for learning (e.g., workshops and courses) and time to experience and digest new ideas and ways of working.[4] That's a lot of time. So while it might at first glance seem to be the best use of time to either schedule some initial training at the beginning of the year and then meet infrequently over the course of the year, or to meet for only short amounts of time every other month or so to "cover" important mentor-related information, this shortened amount of time does not allow mentors to fully gain an understanding of and facility with the important knowledge and skills they need to do their jobs well.

There are some mentoring programs that do not provide much time for mentor professional learning. For example, one of the nations' largest programs, ETS's Pathwise Framework, is very popular right now with schools and districts because it costs less and requires mentors to spend less time in training and more time with teachers. At first glance this seems great—less expensive and more time for mentors to "do their jobs." However, program leaders need to keep in mind that professional learning is a very important part of mentoring work. When professional learning time is scarce, professional development becomes solely about relaying "important" information and accountability, which does not lead to authentic learning and growth. Mentors go into the field less prepared and cannot move teachers as far and as fast as they might be able to do with the proper training. In districts that move to these models, there is an increased sense of dissatisfaction among teachers and mentors, and turnover rates are higher. Many districts that choose Pathwise and other low-professional learning models move back to a more comprehensive model after only a few years. While funds are always an issue, providing enough time to learn to mentor well plays a significant role in the success of mentoring programs.

In an ideal situation, new mentors would participate in an initial series of professional development experiences to introduce them to the complex work of mentoring followed by regular meetings with all mentors as frequently as possible to continue deepening their skills. A calendar might begin something like this:

**Table 2.1. Sample Mentor Professional Development Calendar**

| Month | Professional Development |
|---|---|
| August | • Two to three days of initial training for new mentors<br>• First all-mentor meeting with after meeting for new mentors (one-half day) |
| September | • One to two days of training for new mentors<br>• Weekly/biweekly mentor meetings with after meetings for new mentors (one-half day)<br>• Mentors set goals and create individualized PD plans |
| October | • Weekly/biweekly mentor meetings with after meetings for new mentors (one-half day)<br>• Program leads begin in-field observations of mentors to provide metacoaching and formative feedback related to mentor goals. |
| November | • Weekly/biweekly mentor meetings with after meetings for new mentors (one-half day)<br>• Program leads continue in-field observations of mentors to provide metacoaching and formative feedback related to mentor goals. |

While there is no clear research-based evidence about the amount of time that provides the optimum outcome for mentor professional development, anecdotal reports do make a case that ongoing support—regular, frequent, over multiple years—does seem to make a significant impact on mentor learning and, therefore, on teacher and student learning as well.

## A RIGOROUS PROFESSIONAL
## DEVELOPMENT CURRICULUM

Now that you've carved out a calendar for your mentor professional development, it is time to consider how to spend this precious time with mentors. Most states that support mentoring for new teachers require mentor training but have very little to say about its content or delivery. The few states that do articulate specific training elements include such components as: knowledge of state teaching standards, formative assessment of new teacher performance, classroom observation, and reflective conversations.

Of the thirty-one states that specify mentor training, only fifteen require mentors to have both foundational or initial mentor training and ongoing professional development.[5] While an intensive and structured curriculum of mentor professional development that includes both initial and ongoing training may not be required by many states, ongoing support to deepen and develop mentor knowledge and skill is key to the successful development of an induction program.

When planning a curriculum of mentor professional development, it is important to keep in mind that learning to mentor well takes time. Like many other subjects, there are foundational knowledge and skills needed for successful mentoring that must be learned and then built upon over time as facility with those skills develops. Therefore, planning a multiyear curriculum that differentiates support for mentors at various levels of understanding and proficiency is necessary to consider. The graphic below illustrates a framework for supporting the deepening of mentor knowledge and skill over a multiyear period:

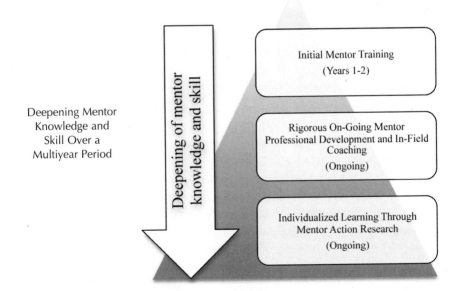

As they begin in their roles, new mentors will need a systematic introduction to the concept of instructional mentoring; the language, processes, and tools mentors use; effective strategies for working with adult learners; and content- or grade-level appropriate mentoring strategies. These can take the form of explicit trainings for new mentors as a group both before beginning the work and periodically throughout their first years.

Then, throughout their tenure, mentors need ongoing support to deepen their knowledge and skills related to the complex work of mentoring. Mentor professional learning might come through regular, guided mentor meetings, wherein all mentors meet on an ongoing basis to learn together. The content of these meetings will vary based on what mentors need at different points in the year and should include time to learn about and practice mentor processes as well as coaching language and skills.

Some programs are using new technologies to support mentors in learning about and reflecting on their practice. For example, in the Fremont Union High School District in Sunnyvale, California, mentors periodically audiorecord their coaching sessions with new teachers. Then, working with each other or the program leader, mentors analyze their conversations, reflect on successful mentoring moves, and consider next steps in their own practice. This mentoring community is also exploring other technologies such as Audacity or AudioNotes that allow both recording and taking notes.[6]

Ongoing mentor learning and support can also come through in-field support, which often takes two forms:

1. Mentors are shadowed during their work with new teachers by program leaders and are provided metacoaching and feedback related to their work with new teachers.
2. Mentors develop coaching partnerships with other mentors who observe each other and provide formative feedback and support for each other.

Mentors also need time to learn about topics that are of importance to them as individuals and that can support their professional growth as a mentor. Goal setting and action research-type experiences done individually and with the mentor learning community can support mentors in further deepening their knowledge and skill in mentoring.

The question then becomes: What are the most important topics and skills to address at each of these phases of mentor development? In a nutshell, successful mentoring requires three sets of skills:

1. knowledge and facility with adult learning theory
2. depth of knowledge and facility with mentoring skills, processes, and language
3. knowledge and facility with content-specific coaching processes

These are not knowledge and skill sets that all classroom teachers, even the really good ones, generally have. Ideally, districts and schools will have the opportunity to select mentors who have some experience working with adult learners and/or coaching others.

Whether or not mentors have had such experiences, all mentors will require training and ongoing support to explicitly develop their skills in working with adults so that they can effectively make the transition from classroom teacher to mentor. They must be explicitly taught and modeled by mentoring program leaders. Mentors must have time to absorb these ideas and practice these skills over time in order to be truly comfortable with them. Let's take a brief look at what each of these skill sets entails and consider how to tailor them to make mentoring work for a specific school or district.

1. *Adult Learning Theory.* Part of being an effective mentor involves understanding how adults learn best. Malcolm Knowles's six principles of adult learning are outlined below along with a brief description of how each impacts mentoring:

- *Adults are internally motivated and self-directed.* Adult learners resist learning when they feel others are imposing information, ideas, or actions on them; therefore, a mentor's job is to facilitate the new teacher's movement toward more self-directed and responsible learning as well as to foster the new teacher's internal motivation to learn. Building trust, showing interest in the new teacher's ideas and opinions, adjusting to the teacher's learning style, setting goals together, engaging in inquiry based on topics of interest to the new teacher, and providing regular constructive and specific feedback can all go a long way toward developing a good working relationship with a new teacher.
- *Adults bring life experiences and knowledge to learning experiences.* Adults like to be given an opportunity to apply their existing knowledge and life experiences to their new learning experiences. Therefore, mentors should work to learn about their new teacher's interests and past experiences (personal and work related), help them draw on those experiences when problem solving, help them reflect and apply new processes, and facilitate reflective learning opportunities that Fidishun suggests can also assist the new

teacher to examine existing biases or habits based on life experiences and "move them toward a new understanding of information presented."[7]

- *Adults are goal oriented.* New teachers become ready to learn when "they experience a need to learn it in order to cope more satisfyingly with real-life tasks or problems."[8] A mentor's role, therefore, is to facilitate a new teacher's readiness for problem-based learning and increase the teacher's awareness of the need for the knowledge or skill presented by providing meaningful learning experiences that are clearly linked to the teacher's personal and professional goals as well as programmatic goals, and by asking questions that motivate reflection, inquiry, and further research.
- *Adults are relevancy oriented.* Adult learners want to know the relevance of what they are learning to what they want to achieve. One way for mentors to help new teachers to see the value of their observations and practical experiences throughout their work together is to ask the new teacher to do some reflection on, for example, what they expect to have happen prior to observing them teach a lesson, on what actually happened and what they learned from that after the observation, and how they might apply what they learned in the future, or how it will help them to meet their learning goals. Mentors can also *provide choices* for new teachers; for example, when giving recommendations for lesson organization, the mentors can provide two or more options, so that lesson is most likely to reflect the new teacher's style and instructional goals.
- *Adults are practical.* During their first years in the classroom, they begin to recognize firsthand how what they learned in their teacher education programs can be practically applied to their work. Mentors should, therefore, clearly explain their reasoning when offering choices about which instructional strategies, assessments, or interventions they would suggest in a particular situation, *be explicit* about how what the mentor and new teacher are discussing is useful and applicable to the particular student or context under consideration, and provide opportunities to practice skills and processes through role-playing, modeling, or through immediate feedback to promote development of skill, confidence, and competence.
- *Adult learners like to be respected.* Mentors can demonstrate respect for new teachers by taking interest; acknowledging the wealth of experiences that the new teacher brings to the work; regarding them as an equal colleague; and encouraging expression of ideas, reasoning, and feedback at every opportunity.[9]

Understanding these key principles of adult learning theory and how they are applicable to mentoring is an important skill set. It takes time to internalize these concepts and to become facile with them in practice. Mentors will need time to absorb these ideas, work together with others to internalize them, play with them during their work with new teachers, and to debrief about the impact of these practices on their mentoring on an ongoing basis.

2. *Mentoring Skills.* In addition to understanding how new teachers learn, mentors need to develop knowledge and skills related to the language, processes, and tools associated with mentoring. One of the biggest challenges many new mentors face is recognizing that the goal of mentoring is not to create in the new teacher a carbon copy of the mentor but, instead, to recognize the new teacher as a unique individual who is capable of developing into an effective teacher who has his or her own unique style separate from the mentor.

The goal of the mentor, therefore, is to use mentoring language, processes, and tools to guide the new teacher in developing to their fullest potential. Mentors must learn how to effectively engage in rich dialogue with new teachers about a wide variety of topics, know when and how to ask questions, know which processes might be most useful to support a teacher's developmental growth, and know when and how to provide the appropriate level of support or guidance.

Gaining mastery of the language and processes of effective mentoring is a difficult and lengthy process. It is not easy, for instance, to figure out where to start with a new teacher, especially when the mentor sees a number of things that need to be addressed and she knows she cannot tackle all of those issues at once. Developing a schema of what is most important to address first and what can wait a little is a valuable, ongoing conversation.

Similarly, capturing objective data when observing classroom interactions is another challenging skill to master. It is easy to have a conceptual understanding of what is "evidence" and what is "opinion," but in practice, this is a much harder concept to master.

Programs that offer mentor training, such as The New Teacher Center, have created useful ways to introduce these and other skills to new mentors. Others, such as Laura Lipton and Bruce Wellman, have created excellent professional development that can support mentors in deepening these skills over time.[10]

Induction programs also often use a set of tools to guide mentoring conversations and to document thinking and learning for record-keeping and/or accreditation purposes. Mentors need time to learn about, practice, and develop facility at using such tools. Being familiar and comfortable with these tools means that mentors can use the tools for recording rich mentoring conversations instead of having the meetings with new teachers be about forms that need to be filled out.

Again, there are excellent packaged mentor tool kits that induction programs can purchase, such as those offered by the New Teacher Center, or induction programs can create their own. Whatever the case, it is imperative the mentors have enough time to learn about and practice with these tools before going out into the field and being asked to use these tools with new teachers.

Supporting mentors in developing and deepening the language, processes, and tools of effective instructional mentoring must be at the heart of ongoing mentor professional development. Program leaders must think about how to continue to support mentors in developing a strong foundation of understanding of these concepts and processes and, at the same time, to not be content with merely a superficial understanding of these processes. They must persist in raising the bar for mentoring excellence and push further toward helping all mentors develop a depth of understanding and a repertoire of skills that is capable of supporting all new teachers in developing to their fullest capacity.

3. *Content-Specific Coaching Processes.* One of the significant differences between buddy mentoring and instructional mentoring is the role of content. Historically, mentoring for new teachers has mainly focused on providing the new teacher with social-emotional and professional socialization support. Helping new teachers deal with the stressful transition period from preservice to teaching and understanding the organizational and professional norms, procedures, and rules that govern the teaching profession and a school or district are important aspects of the mentoring role, but they are not enough. Without a focus on the content knowledge and content-specific instructional skills teachers must know in order to move students' learning forward, mentoring falls short of its true value.

Truly effective mentors need to be more than just good teachers; they also know how to help others to develop the knowledge and skills necessary to be good at teaching content to kids. Therefore, it is imperative that mentors have opportunities to continue to grow their subject matter and subject-specific pedagogical skills as well as learning strategies for tailoring their mentoring work to fit the needs of the content area. Each content area requires different ways of planning, of thinking, and of writing. Mentors who are not familiar with the content area, who don't "think like historians" or "think like scientists," will have a great deal more trouble supporting a new teacher in learning to teach that content, particularly at the secondary level.

Mentoring programs, therefore, need to consider ways that they can support the development of this content- or grade-level specific knowledge and to discuss with others both within and across content areas the modes of mentoring that work best for new teachers within their specific discipline.

## INDIVIDUALIZING MENTOR LEARNING

Mentors are tasked with the important job of growing new teachers' knowledge and skills so they can positively impact student learning. In order to be truly effective at this task, mentors also need to plan for their own learning. However, this is often easier said than done.

Mentors are deeply committed to the learning of others, but they often struggle to make time to grow their own knowledge and skills in a systematic way. Adult learning theory tells us that in order to create the right conditions for mentors to want to learn for themselves, mentors need to be able to set their own meaningful goals based on their areas of genuine interest and curiosity, and be supported in creating a doable plan of action to achieve those goals with support from others. Mentors are usually very busy people, so the goal is to help them find something of genuine interest to them about their mentoring work, help them to understand how improving their knowledge or skill in that area will be beneficial for the new teachers with whom they work, and support them in creating a manageable way to accomplish their goals related to their area of interest.

One way to go about tailoring mentor learning to meet the needs of the mentor is to use teacher action research methodology. Action research is a process in which mentors, teachers, and others engage in a self-directed examination of their own practice systematically and carefully using the techniques of research. It is based on the following assumptions:

- Educators work best on problems they have identified for themselves.
- Educators become more effective when encouraged to examine and assess their own work and then consider ways of working differently.
- Educators help each other by working collaboratively.
- Working with colleagues helps educators in their professional development.

Action research is often done in five phases:

1. Problem Identification
   a. Why do you want to learn about or undertake this task? Is it an important and practical problem, something worth your time and effort, something that could be beneficial to you, your new teachers, and others?
   b. Is the problem stated clearly and in the form of a question? Is it broad enough to allow for a range of insights and findings? Is it narrow enough to be manageable within your time frame and your daily work?

2. Plan of Action
   a. How will you learn about best practices in this area? Is there literature on the subject that might inform your work?
   b. Will you develop and implement a new strategy or approach to address your question? If so, what will it be?
   c. Will you focus your study on existing practices? If so, which particular ones?
   d. What is an appropriate time line for what you are trying to accomplish?

3. Data Collection
   a. What types of data should you try to collect in order to answer your question?
   b. How will you ensure that you have multiple perspectives?
   c. What resources exist, and what information from others might be useful in helping you to frame your question, decide on types of data to collect, or to help you in interpreting your findings?

4. Analysis of Data
   a. What can you learn from the data? What patterns, insights, and new understandings can you find?
   b. What meaning do these patterns, insights, and new understandings have for your practice? For your new teachers? For their students?

5. Plan for Future Action
   a. What will you do differently in your mentoring as a result of this study?
   b. What might you recommend to others?
   c. How will you write/share about what you have learned so that the findings will be useful to you and to others?[11]

These five phases parallel the kind of deeply reflective work we hope mentors and new teachers undertake together in order to grow the new teacher's practice. This parallelism can provide a great jumping-off point for discussions with mentors about the power of continued self-directed learning.

Again, the goal of individualizing mentor learning is to provide just-right professional learning experiences for all mentors, and individual and collective inquiry is a powerful learning process for both mentors and new teachers. However, just as a note of caution, it is important to remember that new mentors have a great deal to learn in their first years and may find it challenging to engage in this more advanced inquiry practice. Therefore, you may find that full-blown action research as described above may be more appropriate for mentors who have completed at least one year of mentor service.

However you decide to go about supporting mentors in continuing to grow their skills and knowledge related to mentoring, it is important to ensure that you create regular time in your curriculum of mentor professional development throughout the year for mentors to work on their own learning. They can:

- informally plan, reflect, and collaborate with other mentors during the formative phases of their action research
- participate in formalized opportunities to share with a small group of colleagues about their plans for work and gain feedback at various stages of the process
- formally share the results of their learning with the rest of the mentor community so that others can benefit from their knowledge and experience

Making space for mentors to engage regularly with their own learning projects as individuals and as a community of learners during mentor meetings, as well as encouraging program leadership to also engage in action research, will elevate the status of this work and ensure that it becomes an important and valued component of mentor professional development.

## MAKING MENTORING WORK FOR YOU

Developing a professional learning program for mentors is a challenging and complex task for induction program leaders. It involves thinking about how to find enough time to create regular and ongoing mentor learning opportunities that support mentors in developing their knowledge and skills over time. It also requires program leaders to weave together learning about adult learning theory, mentoring language, processes, and tools; opportunities to deepen the mentor's knowledge of content and pedagogical content knowledge as well as how to support new teachers in developing their content and pedagogical content knowledge and skills; and to find ways to support mentors in developing the knowledge and skill in areas of personal and professional interest. What might this even look like in practice?

Below is a broad framework for thinking about how to organize mentor professional learning across the year.

Sample Mentor Professional Learning Calendar

| | Initial Mentor Training | Ongoing Mentor Professional Development | Additional Supports for Mentor Learning |
|---|---|---|---|
| Year 1 Mentors | (3-6 days of training): Introduction to mentoring topics, including: <br> • Frameworks governing mentoring work <br> • Adult learning theory <br> • Mentor language, skills, processes <br> • Mentor tools <br> • Teacher leadership | Regular mentor professional development meetings (weekly-monthly), topics include: <br> • Community building <br> • Problem-solving <br> • Continued learning of relevant/new content, skills, strategies, etc. related to grade, content, or school/district initiatives <br> • Deepening understanding of frameworks governing mentoring and how to use them in mentoring interactions <br> • Deepening understanding and facility with mentoring language, skills, processes and tools (including technology) through observation, practice, student work analysis, roleplay, etc. <br> • Setting, working towards, and reflecting on individual professional goals through mentor action research | First year mentors meet with program leadership/lead mentors at least monthly to receive ongoing support on topics of relevance to new mentors. <br><br> Program leads or other veteran mentors provide in-field support for new mentors at least once during the year. Formative feedback is provided in relation to mentor goals and program standards. |
| Year 2 Mentors | (3-6 days of training): Advanced mentoring topics, including: <br> • Tailoring mentoring to meet the needs of all students <br> • Addressing issues of equity <br> • Dealing with challenging situations | | Program leads or other veteran mentors provide in-field support for mentors at least once during the year. Formative feedback is provided in relation to mentor goals and program standards. |
| Year 3 + Mentors | (2-4 days of training): Mentors select from a range of choices offered by the program, the district, or through another venue to develop their skills. Topics could include: <br> • Advanced mentoring language or skill work <br> • Topics relevant to the current instructional focus of the school/district <br> • Topics of their own choosing relevant to the mentoring role/self-selected goals | | Program leads or other veteran mentors provide in-field support for mentors at least once during the year. Feedback is provided in relation to mentor goals and program standards. |

Of note in this framework are the differentiated supports for mentors at various levels of development. Note that new mentors receive initial training, additional support during mentor professional development, and increased in-field support and feedback. More veteran mentors have the opportunity to choose their professional development. All mentors attend mentor professional development meetings, but learning opportunities and support during these meetings may also be differentiated to address the various levels of facility with material and tools being discussed or by grade level/content to provide the most relevant fit possible for each mentor.

It can also be helpful for program leadership to develop a detailed "curriculum map" of each mentor-learning experience throughout the year to outline the sequence of support over the course of the year and to ensure all relevant and important pieces are included at the right time of the year to best support mentors.

By creating an intensive and structured curriculum of professional learning that is tailored to meet mentors' developmental and individualized needs and is provided in a timely, regular, and ongoing manner, induction program leaders will increase mentor capacity to do the important work of instructional mentoring.

Below is a list of the big ideas about the creation of effective mentor professional learning that were described in this chapter for you to consider as you move your program forward:

- Create regular and ongoing mentor-learning opportunities both in mentor meetings and in the field that support mentors in developing their knowledge and skills over time.
- Provide regular opportunities for mentors to learn about adult learning theory, mentoring language, processes, and tools.
- Provide regular opportunities for mentors to deepen their content and pedagogical content knowledge as well as how to support new teachers in developing their content and pedagogical content knowledge skills.
- Differentiate mentor support for mentors at various levels of development and with varying levels of personal and professional interest.
- Develop a detailed "curriculum map" of mentor learning experiences.

## READY TO TAKE THE NEXT STEP?

At the end of this section, there is a Discussion Guide designed to help program leaders consider the key ideas discussed in this chapter. These questions are designed to support you in beginning the important discussions about these key topics with other stakeholders and decision makers in your organization.

## NOTES

1. Hayes Mizell, "Why Professional Development Matters," *Learning Forward.* Oxford, OH: 2010. Accessed from: http://www.learningforward.org/docs/pdf/why_pd_matters_web.pdf.

2. Barry L. Bull, Mark Buechler, Steve Didley, and Lee Krehbiel, "Professional Development and Teacher Time: Principles, Guidelines, and Policy Options for Indiana." Bloomington, IN: Indiana Education Policy Center, School of Educations, Indiana University, 1994; Tom C. Corcoran, "Transforming Professional Development for Teachers: A Guide for State Policymakers." Washington, DC: National Governors Association, 1995; Thomas R. Guskey, "Professional Development in Education: In Search of the Optimal Mix." Paper presented at the Annual Meeting of the American Educational Research Association, New Orleans, Louisiana, 1994.

3. Joseph Cambone, "Time for Teachers in School Restructuring." *Teachers College Record* 96, no. 3 (1995): 512–43; Corcoran, "Transforming Professional Development for Teachers"; V. Troen and K. Boles, "Two Teachers Examine the Power of Teacher Leadership." In *Teachers as Leaders: Perspectives on the Professional Development of Teachers,* edited by D. R. Walling, 275–86. Bloomington, IN: Phi Delta Kappa Educational Foundation, 1994; G. D. Watts and S. Castle, "The Time Dilemma in School Restructuring." *Phi Delta Kappan* 75, no. 4 (1993): 306–10.

4. Cambone, "Time for Teachers in School Restructuring."

5. New Teacher Center, "State Policy Reviews." Santa Cruz, CA: Author, 2014. Accessed from: http://www.newteachercenter.org/policy/policy-map.

6. Josh Maisel (Fremont Union High School District Induction Program director) in conversation with the author, January 2014.

7. Delores Fidishun, "Andragogy and Technology: Integrating Adult Learning Theory as We Teach Technology." *Proceedings of the 2000 Mid-South Instructional Technology Conference.* Murfreesboro, TN: Middle Tennessee State University, April 2000, 4.

8. Malcolm S. Knowles, *The Modern Practice of Adult Education: From Pedagogy to Andragogy.* Englewood Cliffs: Prentice Hall/Cambridge, 1980, 44.

9. Malcolm S. Knowles, Elwood F. Holton III, and Richard A. Swanson. *The Adult Learner.* New York: Routledge, 2012.

10. Laura Lipton, Bruce Wellman, and Carrlette Humbard. *Mentoring Matters: A Practical Guide To Learning Focused Relationships.* Charlotte, VT: MiraVia, LLC, 2003.

11. Adapted from the work of Fairfax County Public Schools, Office of Research and Policy Analysis, and the St. Louis Action Research Evaluation Committee.

# 3

# Strategic Deployment of Mentors

## Emily Davis and Betty Achinstein

| Well Developed |
|---|
| *New teachers are consistently matched with mentors knowledgeable about how to teach their subject matter and/or grade level to all students.* |
| *New teachers are consistently matched with mentors knowledgeable about the school/context/students where the new teacher is working.* |

At the heart of a package of supports for new teachers is a high-quality mentor. Studies have shown that when new teachers are given regular time to meet with a mentor who is knowledgeable, these interactions can have a statistically significant impact on new teacher retention as well as on teacher practice and student learning.

There are many definitions of a highly skilled coach. A favorite comes from Jim Knight, in a presentation he gave to the National Staff Development Conference in 2008, where he said a quality coach:

1. is an equal peer, who provides choice and voice to new teachers as adult learners and helps them engage in meaningful reflection and dialogue about their practice to achieve praxis
2. has a deep understanding of the proven instructional practices they share with teachers, particularly around classroom management, content enhancement, instruction, and assessment for learning
3. understands and uses the components of coaching and uses a language of ongoing regard with the new teachers to provide constructive feedback based on data to help shape the teachers' practice
4. is an effective relationship builder who seeks out an affirmation point, looks for common denominators, is empathetic, engages in conversation, and listens
5. balances ambition with humility
6. spends more than 50 percent of his/her time focused on content and directly improving instruction[1]

When coaching is done well, the result is student achievement that can be seen both by the coach and the teacher.

Jim Knight's description of high-quality mentoring represents an ideal. Unfortunately, few induction programs can claim that their mentors are/ do all of these things consistently. While many programs do support mentors in learning to develop in some of these areas, not all of them are equally valued. This may be because of the historic roles that mentors have filled in schools and in the lives of teachers.

The kind of support mentors provide generally falls into two categories: emotional or psychological support, and support that focuses on instruction.[2] Over the past twenty years, the primary goal of mentoring has been to help teachers deal with the stressful transition into the profession and to address the high rates of teacher turnover that often occur during the first five years of teaching. In order to support teachers during this critical period, mentors have been tasked with working primarily in the psychological support realm by providing socioemotional support and professional socialization.

Through the socioemotional support role, the mentor becomes a caretaker of the new teacher. They provide emotional adjustment and self-image support for the novice teacher, and they engage in advice giving, story swapping, and counseling.[3] The goal of the socioemotional support role is to help normalize this often-traumatic adjustment period, which Veenman describes as "transition shock," or "praxisshock,"[4] and to support novice teachers in gaining the confidence they need to continue in the profession.

The goal of the professional socialization role, which has also been called career functions support, is to induct new teachers into the norms, rules, and routines of "how we do things" in this profession and in this school. In this role, the mentor becomes the local guide enculturating the novice into school and district policies, and he or she focuses on the technical aspects of teaching in general, such as classroom management.[5]

These two roles are incredibly important ones for mentors to play in the lives of new teachers, especially during this challenging phase of new teachers' careers. They are greatly valued by beginning teachers and may help reduce attrition.[6] New teachers consistently comment on how valuable their mentors were because the mentors listened, helped them problem solve, and were a shoulder to cry on when they needed them. As Laura Lipton writes, "emotional safety is necessary to produce cognitive complexity,"[7] meaning that the kind of social and emotional support a mentor provides is necessary because it creates a safe space for truly deep work to be done together.

There is no doubt this kind of social and emotional support is truly important for new teachers as they navigate the incredible challenges of beginning to teach independently, and the expectation should be that mentors know and understand these roles and how to fulfill them for the novice teachers with whom they work. The question becomes, however, are these the only roles mentors should serve? Given the current educational climate, is it enough for mentors to only be cheerleaders and tour guides? What is missing from this picture?

This chapter will explore two key considerations mentoring program leaders should have in mind when matching mentors and new teachers:

1. content-alike mentoring
2. context-alike mentoring

## CONTENT-ALIKE MENTORING

The current political environment surrounding schools suggests that the socioemotional and professionalization mentoring roles may no longer be enough. Currently, there are two educational movements underway that would indicate a need for a change:

1. the current era of high-stakes testing as well as the rise of ambitious new teaching goals such as common core standards, and
2. heightened accountability for teachers to ensure student progress against these standards.

This renewed focus on content learning and the increasing pressure on teachers to know how to support all students in achieving these standards calls for a revision of thinking about the role of the mentor in the life of the novice teacher. The intersection of these two movements suggests there is a third role for mentors focused on the subject matter novices must teach.

To improve their pedagogical knowledge and skill, new teachers also need support focused on the core of education—teaching and learning content. In fact, a number of studies have found that when new teachers receive content-focused mentoring from someone with disciplinary knowledgeable experience, they experience more positive outcomes for both teachers and students than those who only receive emotional support. They are more likely to continue teaching in their schools of origin[8] and to develop a deeper understanding of the nature of the subject and its representation in the classroom and use more inquiry-oriented lessons, student-centered practices, and reform-based instruction.[9]

For example, in a study of various induction programs for new science teachers, Julie Luft found that science-specific induction programs show promise in helping new teachers continue building and solidifying their discipline (e.g., general science, biology, chemistry) or topic (e.g., heat, motion), Pedagogical Content Knowledge (PCK), and continue using science teaching practices consistent with National Science Education Standards.[10] Further, Julie Luft and Nancy Patterson found that:

> By making general topics more science specific, like classroom management, beginning teachers were able to apply the suggestions immediately to their own instructional setting. In addition, the specialized support program reinforced theories and practices espoused during the science component of initial certification programs, and grounded current classroom experiences within the framework of the National Science Education Standards.[11]

Matching a novice with a mentor who is knowledgeable in their discipline has also been shown to have significant positive results on student achievement,[12] thus highlighting the importance of developing new teacher's subject-specific knowledge and practice.

There may have been some hesitation to task mentors with this important role in the past because it was assumed that novice teachers entered the profession already having mastered the content either in their undergraduate or teacher education programs and, therefore, do not need mentor support in this area. However, especially in our most high-need schools and districts, many novices enter teaching with little preparation or content knowledge, and even those that have completed full preparation and have content knowledge still need to learn how to teach content to students in context—to develop pedagogical content knowledge, and to understand how topics are organized, represented, and adapted to particular student learners and contexts.[13] This makes the need for mentoring that is focused on novices' development of content and pedagogical content knowledge all the more important, particularly in districts and schools where new teachers may enter with little previously applicable content and teaching background.

There are also a number of challenges that arise for mentors when subject matter enters the picture. For example, mentors themselves often lack the knowledge to guide novices in developing content-specific teaching. As induction programs rarely prioritize matching novices and mentors by grade or content area, mentors are often matched with a novice teacher who works outside his or her area of expertise and, so, may not know how to support the new teacher's content growth. While mentors may have a strong repertoire of general pedagogical and instructional knowledge they can share with teachers across content and grade levels, this mismatch usually leads to mentoring conversations that focus on generic topics such as teaching, students, management, and assessment in isolation without the important framework of content that can tie these topics together and lead to more complex and deep discussions about how these topics relate to one another. As a result, there is surprisingly little discussion about content happening in mentoring exchanges.

For example, in a study of sixteen pairs of novice elementary teachers and their mentors in California, Michael Strong and Wendy Baron found that only 2 percent of mentor suggestions focused on subject matter. While the authors note elementary teachers are not subject specialists, they do report surprise at the lack of subject talk given the importance of content in the California Standards for the Teaching Profession.[14]

Perhaps the challenges described above only reinforce mentors' roles as emotional supporters and socialization guides, and limit mentor's ability or willingness to take on a subject-focused role that could impact teacher and student learning.

So what would a mentor who is matched with a new teacher by content be able to do with a new teacher that a mentor whose background is in another subject could not? Let's take secondary history as an example.

One current goal of teaching history is to help students learn to "think like a historian" by learning the skills professional historians use to investigate historical questions. To do so, students need to learn to use discipline-specific reading strategies such as sourcing, contextualizing, corroborating, and close reading to critically examine and analyze information from primary and secondary sources. This method aligns well with the literacy goals outlined in the Common Core but is often challenging for new history teachers to develop as it marks a change from traditional history curriculums that focus primarily on memorization of discrete dates and facts.

A history-specific mentor can help the new teacher to consider how to organize not only their content into units and lessons (thematically? chronologically?) but also weave through them the teaching of these important historical literacy skills. The content-knowledgeable mentor might be familiar with the "Reading Like a Historian" curriculum developed by the Stanford History Education Group, which has created units to teach these skills already and that can be accessed for free on the Internet.[15] She might also know and use as a cornerstone of her interactions with new history teachers the core teaching practices identified by history education researcher Brad Fogo, which describe nine key areas history teachers need to develop in their practice.[16]

While a mentor with an English background might be able to support this new teacher in thinking about teaching reading and writing generally, the way in which these skills are described and used in a history classroom is significantly different than the way similar skills are used in an English classroom. If the mentor has a math background, she might not even be able to provide this level of content-specific support. In addition, the general mentor cannot help the new teacher to decide on which key terms and events are most important to consider or which often confuse students. She also cannot help the new teacher to consider possible organizational concepts for history education, and she cannot easily locate primary sources, media, colleagues, and other resources to plan lessons. (For a content-specific example from math, please see chapter 9.)

Mentors who possess content-specific knowledge and pedagogy speak and understand the language of the discipline in a way others do not. They can support a new teacher in developing both their content knowledge and their discipline-specific instructional skills and connect them to valuable resources and colleagues. When the mentor does not speak the language of the content, mentors often rely upon the new teacher to be content experts. New teachers must then spend precious time attempting to explain the content to their mentors so that they can discuss how to plan it. Even then, the instructional methodologies mentors suggest may not align with the best practices suggested by their disciplines, meaning that instead of confirming and strengthening what they learned in their preparation programs, general mentors inadvertently support the development of less effective teaching habits in teachers.

## CONTEXT-ALIKE MENTORING

In addition to being matched with a mentor who is knowledgeable about the subject matter the new teacher is teaching, mentors should also have knowledge and experience about the context in which the new teacher is working; namely, their school or district and student population.

Mentors who have previously worked in the school where a new teacher is assigned bring with them a significant body of knowledge about the way a school works as well as the goals and priorities of the administration. They know the staff, which can allow mentors to help new teachers make connections with knowledgeable and helpful others. They are also familiar with the students and know the strengths and needs of the student population, which allows the mentor to help the new teacher plan effective lessons and navigate potential challenges in ways that someone outside of that school might not be able to do.

Currently or recently working in a school where a new teacher is employed can be helpful in some ways, but it may be a huge challenge for an educator to mentor in a school where he/she has recently taught as former roles and relationships with faculty and administration are tough to forget. Whereas in the past, mentors may have shared confidential information with a principal with whom they were close, in their new relationship they must keep their work with the new teachers confidential. This can cause stress on the new mentor-administrator relationship.

As further evidence of the value context-specific knowledge can have for a mentoring relationship, Jonah Rockoff's study of the New York City's Induction Program found that the mentor's previous experience in a school seems to play a significant role in new teachers' perceptions of mentor effectiveness.[17]

Instead, some schools and districts are rethinking what they mean by context-specific matching. Perhaps knowledge of the district is enough to provide context-specific support. Having taught in the district, the mentor understands the mission, vision, and goals of the district, understands its structure and hierarchies, and knows the students and communities. In Durham, North Carolina, for example, mentors are never assigned to the school in which they most immediately taught but are reassigned to support new teachers in the district. Program leaders there feel this is enough to both provide context-specific support and to allow the mentor to reestablish themselves in their new role without having to navigate previous relationships with school leaders and colleagues on a daily basis.[18]

Savvy mentoring program leaders will recognize that when mentors have both knowledge of subject matter and of the students with whom a new teacher is working, they are set up for mentoring success. When schools and districts are spending time, funding, and other resources to provide mentoring support for new teachers, not to mention pulling some of our best teachers out of the classroom to be mentors, shouldn't they want to ensure that they are getting the most bang for their buck? Deploying mentors based on content and context seems to be the best way to make the most of the resources at our disposal.

## WHEN CONTENT- AND CONTEXT-ALIKE MATCHING JUST ISN'T AN OPTION

As seen in the previous sections, the research all indicates that matching new teachers with mentors who understand their context and content ensures mentoring programs are making the most of the knowledge and skills mentors have. But what if this just isn't possible in your school or district? A program operating in a single school or small district may not have the luxury of employing content- and context-specific mentors because of scale. For example, there may only be five new science teachers, which is not enough to fill a full-release mentor's caseload in a single school. Or, perhaps there are thirteen new science teachers in the district, but they are spread out across ten schools. In this case, the mentor cannot possibly understand the context of each of the schools and must travel significant distances to meet with the various science teachers. All this travel time could greatly erode the "acting" time a mentor has with a teacher.

In these situations, program leaders have to make choices about how best to deploy their mentors. Should the program fully release a mentor in the school where there are five new science teachers as well as a new English teacher, a new math teacher, and a new PE teacher? This mentor would understand the context of the school and can provide general instructional, curricular, and management support for these new teachers, but they could not provide content-specific support for all of the new teachers. Or should the program fully release a mentor with science content knowledge to serve all the new science teachers in the district? This mentor would be able to support the new science teachers with content, but they would not be able to provide the context-specific support that someone in their school might be able to offer.

There are ways to ensure that new teachers, even in single schools or small districts, can have mentors who have some knowledge about both their content and context. However, these models require other tradeoffs. One program in a rural Virginia school district, for example, operates a one-to-one mentoring program. In this model, mentors have no release time from their teaching duties but only provide mentoring support to one new teacher in their department. In this situation, mentors have both content- and context-specific knowledge and skills to share with their new teachers. However, because the mentors have no release time, they do not have the opportunity to observe new teachers, and they often cannot meet with new teachers during the school day because they lack a common prep. These mentors also do not have time in their schedules to attend regular mentor professional development, and so they may not be as skilled as their partial- or full-release counterparts who can participate in regular learning experiences.

In one large urban district in Florida, mentors are fully released from their classrooms and are not matched to new teachers by level (elementary, middle, high), but an attempt is made to make a content match. The program leads made the decision that a full-release model best fit the need of their large urban district and allowed them to build in professional development time so the mentors could have time to learn to mentor well. Program leaders also decided that the best use of their mentors was to assign them to work in a limited number of schools within a small geographical area in order to develop deeper relationships in the school and to reduce time lost in the travel from school to school.

The tradeoff is that the mentors may not have the grade-specific knowledge or the school-specific knowledge, but they can provide content-specific support and they can work to develop context-specific knowledge over time as they spend time in these schools getting to know the teachers, students, and administrators. This program also chooses not to assign mentors to the school where they most immediately taught. This is an intentional choice to help support the creation of the mentor identity. If the mentor taught in the school, that mentor, for an extended time, will be remembered as a teacher and the relationships nurtured as a teacher. All of those relationships are subject to change in the mentor role, and it is especially hard for the mentor and principal to navigate the confidentiality issue if that had not governed their prior work together.

The Fremont Union High School district in Sunnyvale, California, on the other hand, uses a model that prioritizes context-alike mentoring. Program leaders feel the knowledge mentors have of a specific school is more valuable than the content-specific pedagogy they might have. In this model, mentors are paired with all the new teachers in a specific school, regardless of content area. Mentors are chosen for their strong pedagogical skills that can be shared across a wide range of content areas, and then the mentors work together as a team to support each other in addressing any content-specific needs that might arise. The development of a strong mentoring team deployed by context but with a wide range of content knowledge to support each other meets the needs of this particular district.[19]

Matching new teachers by context and content is ideal, but is not always an option. Program leaders need to carefully consider the tradeoffs that matching new teachers to mentors without content- or context-specific knowledge might have and make educated decisions about how best to deploy their mentors.

## MAKING MENTORING WORK FOR YOU

Working with a highly skilled mentor can have a significant impact on new teacher's retention and development as well as on the learning of students, but mentoring alone is not enough to ensure the success of a new teacher. To truly be successful in the teaching profession, teachers need to build connections with a community of colleagues who will continue to provide ongoing professional support and guidance long after the short term of mentoring has passed. We will explore these other connections in the next two sections of this chapter. Below is a list of recommendations related to the strategic deployment of mentors:

1. A knowledgeable mentor needs to know how to provide socioemotional and professional socialization support for novice teachers, but that is not enough.
2. Districts need to consider how to prioritize matching mentors and novices by content and grade level to ensure a more efficient match or to consider the tradeoffs that occur when this type of mentor-novice matching cannot occur.

3. It should not be assumed that good teachers know how to be content mentors. They need training and support (more on this in the mentoring professional development section).
4. Assigning mentors to work with teachers in their school or district where they taught can add significant value to mentoring.

## READY TO TAKE THE NEXT STEP?

At the end of this section, there is a Discussion Guide designed to help program leaders consider the key ideas discussed in this chapter. These questions are designed to support you in beginning the important discussions about these key topics with other stakeholders and decision makers in your organization.

## NOTES

1. Jim Knight, "Instructional Coaching: What We Are Learning about Effective Coaching Practices." Presentation to the National Staff Development Conference, Orlando, Florida, December 6, 2008.

2. Yvonne Gold, "Beginning Teacher Support: Attrition, Mentoring, and Induction." In *Handbook of Research on Teacher Education* 2, edited by John Sikula, T. Buttery, and E. Guyton, 548–94. New York: Macmillan, 1996.

3. Ibid.; Jian Wang and Sandra J. Odell, "Mentored Learning to Teach According to Standards-Based Reform: A Critical Review." *Review of Educational Research* 72, no. 3 (2002): 481–546; Betty Achinstein and Steven Z. Athanases, "Mentoring New Teachers for Equity and the Needs of English Language Learners." In *Past, Present and Future Research on Teacher Induction: An Anthology for Researchers, Policy Makers, and Practitioners*, edited by Jian Wang, Sandra Odell, and Renee Clift, 187–204. Commission on Teacher Induction and Mentoring, Association of Teacher Educators: Rowman & Littlefield Education.

4. Simon Veenman, "Perceived Problems of Beginning Teachers." *Review of Educational Research* 54, no. 2 (1984): 143.

5. Achinstein and Athanases, "Mentoring New Teachers for Equity and the Needs of English Language Learners"; Sharon Feiman-Nemser and Margaret Buchmann, "When Is Student Teaching Teacher Education?" *Teaching and Teacher Education* 3, no. 4 (1987): 255–73; Patrick M. Shields, Camille E. Esch, Daniel C. Humphrey, Viki M. Young, Margaret Gaston, and Harvey Hunt, "The Status of the Teaching Profession: Research Findings and Policy Recommendations. A Report to the Teaching and California's Future Task Force." *The Center for the Future of Teaching and Learning*, Santa Cruz, CA: 1999; Veenman, "Perceived Problems of Beginning Teachers."

6. Sandra J. Odell and Douglas P. Ferraro, "Teacher Mentoring and Teacher Retention." *Journal of Teacher Education* 43, no. 3 (1992): 200–04.

7. Laura Lipton, Bruce Wellman, and Carlette Humbard, *Mentoring Matters: A Practical Guide to Learning-Focused Relationships*. Charlotte, VT: MiraVia, LLC, 2003.

8. Thomas Smith and Richard Ingersoll, "What Are the Effects of Induction and Mentoring on Beginning Teacher Turnover?" *American Educational Research Journal* 41, no. 3 (2004): 681–714.

9. Julie A. Luft, Gillian H. Roehrig, and Nancy C. Patterson, "Contrasting Landscapes: A Comparison of the Impact of Different Induction Programs on Beginning Secondary Science Teachers' Practices, Beliefs, and Experiences." *Journal of Research in Science Teaching* 40, no. 1 (2003): 77–97; Jian Wang, Michael Strong, and Sandra J. Odell, "Mentor-Novice Conversations about Teaching: A Comparison of Two U.S. and Two Chinese Cases." *Teacher College Record* 106, no. 4 (2004): 775–813.

10. Julie A. Luft, "Beginning Secondary Science Teachers in Different Induction Programmes: The First Year of Teaching." *International Journal of Science Education* 31, no. 17 (2009): 2355–84.

11. Julie A. Luft and Nancy C. Patterson, "Bridging the Gap: Supporting Beginning Science Teachers." *Journal of Science Teacher Education* 13, no. 4 (2002): 267–82.

12. Jonah E. Rockoff, "Does Mentoring Reduce Turnover and Improve Skills of New Employees? Evidence from Teachers in New York City" (Working Paper 13868). Cambridge, MA: National Bureau of Economic Research, 2008. Accessed from: www.nber.org/papers/w13868; Donald J. Boyd, Pam Grossman, Hamilton Lankford, Susanna Loeb, Matthew Ronfeldt, and Jim Wyckoff, "Recruiting Effective Math Teachers: Evidence from New York City." *American Educational Research Journal* 49, no. 6 (2012): 1008–47.

13. Lee S. Shulman, "Knowledge and Teaching: Foundations of the New Reform." *Harvard Educational Review* 57, no. 1 (1987): 1–23.

14. Michael Strong and Wendy Baron, "An Analysis of Mentoring Conversations with Beginning Teachers: Suggestions and Responses." *Teaching and Teacher Education* 20, no. 1 (2004): 47–57.

15. Stanford.edu, Reading Like a Historian. Accessed from: http://sheg.stanford.edu/rlh.

16. Stanford.edu, Center to Support Excellence in Teaching. Accessed from: https://cset.stanford.edu/research/core-practices.

17. Rockoff, "Does Mentoring Reduce Turnover and Improve Skills of New Employees?"

18. Fred Williams (former Durham, North Carolina, Induction Program director) in conversation with the author, January 2014.

19. Josh Maisel (Fremont Union High School District Induction Program director) in conversation with the author, January 2014.

# 4

# Protected and Well-Used
# Mentoring Time

**Well Developed**

*Protected time is provided for mentors and new teachers to regularly meet with and observe new teachers (1.5 hours per week/6-8 hours per month).*

*Mentors spend the majority of their time with new teachers engaged in rigorous mentoring processes that will improve immediate and long-term instruction and student learning.*

*New teachers are rigorously mentored for at least two years.*

Time also matters. We know from the professional development literature that effective teacher learning happens when it is organized in a sustained and coherent manner, it takes place during the school day, it becomes part of a teacher's professional responsibilities, and it focuses on student results.[1] These tenets also hold true for induction as a form of professional development.

To illustrate this point, let's look at a series of studies undertaken between 2001 and 2006 by several groups of researchers that used survey data, achievement scores, and several other variables to understand the impact of mentoring in New York City, the largest school district in the nation, which employs roughly seven thousand new teachers and three hundred to five hundred mentors in any given year. In this induction program, mentors are expected to spend an average of 1.5 hours with each new teacher each week over the period of one year.

Each of the research teams found that some mentors spent more time with new teachers than recommended, and some less. They also were consistent in their finding that having more time with a mentor increases the novice's satisfaction with mentoring.[2] Jonah Rockoff writes, "Teachers who received more hours of mentoring gave better evaluations of their mentors. On average, evaluations rose by 0.19 standard deviations when hours of mentoring increased by 10."[3] He further suggests that additional hours of mentoring raised teacher evaluations of the quality of service. Further, the researchers concluded that more time with a mentor led to an increase in student achievement in both reading and math and to an increase in teacher retention.[4]

While these findings are very positive, the researchers do note that the New York City induction program has a few concerning features related to the time with a mentor:

1. The caseload of new teachers for each mentor is approximately 17:1, which is higher than recommended due to budgetary constraints. This may lead to a decrease in contact time with each new teacher and, therefore, may reduce the effectiveness and perception of support for new teachers.[5]
2. Due to budgetary issues, the New York City induction program only supports teachers in their first year, so after one year of increase, the impact of mentoring tends to level or drop off considerably.[6]

The data from these studies clearly indicates that more time for mentoring leads to an increase in the effectiveness of induction activities in terms of teacher retention, teacher and student learning, and student achievement. However, one of the most difficult challenges for any induction program, including the one in New York City, is finding time and funding to make mentoring happen often enough and for a long enough period when teachers, schools, and districts have so many pressing responsibilities to which teachers must attend.

So how can we make the most of mentoring time? This chapter will explore three key factors that can increase the success of time with a mentor:

- contact time
- intensity
- duration

## CONTACT TIME

Many researchers, including Jonah Rockoff and Pamela Grossman, consistently note that one of the design elements of induction programs that is most associated with teaching effectiveness and student learning is the frequency and duration of mentor–new teacher contact. They note that frequent and substantive interactions help mentors and new teachers to develop a mentoring relationship and provide beginning teachers the unencumbered time they need to reflect on their teaching under the guidance of a knowledgeable other in order to grow in their craft.

Yet research suggests that many teachers often don't get as much time with a mentor as their induction program mandates or as the new teacher desires or needs[7] either due to late assignment, high mentor caseloads, school/context time constraints, or other factors. Without this time, programmatic intent is undermined and the likelihood of improved new teacher effectiveness and student achievement is greatly lessened.

To punctuate this message, the New Teacher Center recommends 1.5 hours per week or six to eight hours per month of "protected time for interactions between the mentor and mentee."[8] It is important to keep in mind that the ideal amount of time for each new teacher will vary greatly, and that programs should not mandate a specific amount of time for each meeting. Instead, offering a range of time, such as the above at six to eight hours a month, is an appropriate and useful practice. This allows mentors to flex to the needs of the new teacher while still ensuring that each new teacher has enough time with their mentor to pursue their own growth.

These time frames are also important to specify when sharing program requirements with school administrators and other partners. Unless specific requirements around time are in place, competing priorities at the school site will overshadow time for interactions between mentors and new teachers. This often yields limited or no time for meaningful instructional conversations and classroom observations, and therefore it diminishes (or negates altogether) effects on student and teacher outcomes.

We also know that this time with a mentor needs to occur during school hours and should not be expected to take place outside of the school day. This means that induction programs must make sure that beginners' time is not filled with other activities that have little relationship to their teaching, that leave little room for their immediate concerns, or that deny them a reasonable personal life.

## INTENSITY

While having significant regular time with a mentor is important for increasing new teacher effectiveness, simply having the time together is not enough. Even when mentors and new teachers are matched by content (see the section in chapter 3 on content-specific mentoring), it does not guarantee that new teachers will receive the support they need to effectively grow their practice. Mentors and program leaders need to consider what mentors and new teachers do together during that time that will lead to increased new teacher knowledge and effectiveness in the classroom.

In order to be a successful content-mentoring experience, the mentor and new teacher need to spend at least 50 percent of their time talking about content and how to teach content to all students. Ten years of research shows that mentors typically spend only 25 percent of their time on improving instruction.[9] While instruction is a more general topic than talking about content and content-specific pedagogy, the point is still clear that without spending at least half their time talking about teaching and learning, mentors are still only filling the socioemotional and professional socialization roles.

Instead, mentoring conversations need to focus on the key aspects of learning to teach academic content. Lee Shulman talked about a need to focus, not just on the expert knowledge of a particular content area (i.e., the axioms, formulas, and ideas of mathematics), but on the way students learn content. He coined the phrase *pedagogical content knowledge* to describe the specialized knowledge teachers need to effectively convey content to students, such as the knowledge to select appropriate models to illustrate new concepts as well as knowledge of learners and their characteristics.

Moreover, Shulman said we must distinguish content knowledge (knowledge of subject matter) and pedagogical content knowledge (knowledge of how to teach subject matter to students) from general pedagogical knowledge (knowledge of teaching strategies, classroom management, and organization across content areas). He convincingly argued that, to teach successfully, teachers must have a deep and meaningful understanding of the content they teach, as well as how students learn that content, including common misunderstandings.[10]

So what should mentors and novice teachers spend their content-focused time exploring? Sharon Feiman-Nemser and Michelle Parker provided this concise list:

- learning to represent/present academic content
- learning to think about subject matter and students' perspectives
- deepening the novice's subject-matter understanding
- learning to organize students for the teaching and learning of content[11]

To accelerate new teacher learning and instructional practice, mentors need to make sure they are doing more than just providing emotional support or socialization into the norms of the school and profession. Instead, they need to ensure that they are spending their precious time with new teachers engaged in conversations that will lead to improved teaching and learning for both the new teacher and her students.

## DURATION

Research also tells us that even the best one-year program is not enough. The effects of induction begin to drop off after a program ends, and new teacher practice begins to regress to the norm. With only one year of support under their belt, new teachers often do not have all the tools in place they need to continue to accelerate their own learning and, therefore, the learning of their students.

In a study by Steven Glazerman and colleagues, the researchers report that having a mentor for at least two years dramatically increases the effectiveness of mentoring.[12] This amount of time increases the likelihood that new teachers will have developed their knowledge and instructional skills as well as their understanding about how to continue to grow their practice long after their time with their mentor is over. While there continues to be some regression to the mean even after a two-year or longer program, the new teacher begins at a much higher level of competence and knows how to keep himself or herself moving forward to a greater degree than those with less lengthy support.

Induction programs should also consider what supports follow induction for teachers as they continue into their career. Ideally, schools and districts would create a cohesive pipeline of teacher learning that extends from preservice, through induction, into career-long professional development. For example, Stanford University's Teacher Education Program is working in conjunction with the Woodrow Wilson Fellowship program to create a four-year system of support that begins during preservice, continues through two years of content-focused mentoring support, and culminates by beginning the National Boards for Professional Certification program. This pipeline of support that continues to push teachers toward excellence can ensure teachers never stop learning or improving their practice, which is a worthy goal for all who work to develop teachers to their fullest potential.

## MAKING MENTORING WORK FOR YOU

Time is an incredibly important factor in the success of an induction program. To maximize the success of mentoring, program leaders will need to consider how to find the resources that will allow teachers and mentors to spend a significant amount of time together on a regular basis over an extended period of time. Below are some recommendations for program leaders related to time:

1. Create non-negotiables about time. This could include quantifying a minimum amount or narrow range of time mentors and new teachers spend together, or could include creating robust requirements for mentor performance and program standards that explicitly require sufficient time and for mentor-mentee interactions. Make sure stakeholders are educated about the impact time has on programmatic success and are involved in writing these guidelines so everyone is on the same page about this important priority from the beginning.
2. Think carefully about mentor caseloads. When mentors are assigned too many new teachers to support, there are not physically enough hours in a given day or week for a mentor to spend the necessary amount of time with each of them. As a result, some organizations and programs recommend no more than a 16:1 ratio. Creating caseloads smaller than that ensures sufficient time. However, it is also important to remember that more veteran mentors may have developed the skills and processes to successfully support more new teachers than new mentors might. It is also important to weigh the needs of new teachers entering the program, as some might need more support than others, and this might affect caseloads.
3. Work with schools to create sanctioned time for interactions between mentors and beginning teachers that may not be co-opted for other "more pressing" school matters. Mentors and new teachers need to be assured that they have some set time each week to interact in addition to time spent in classrooms working with students.
4. Make sure new teachers in need of induction are assigned to a mentor caseload in a timely manner. Ideally, this means mentors and new teachers meet prior to the start of the year, not weeks/months into the school year.
5. Ensure mentors are prioritizing their content role and spend at least 50 percent of time talking about content with novices in order to truly support the novice's content knowledge and skill growth.
6. Work to find funding that will help your program stretch beyond one year and will become part of a seamless teacher professional development pipeline that extends from preservice through induction and throughout a teacher's career to build excellent career-long learners.

## READY TO TAKE THE NEXT STEP?

At the end of this section, there is a Discussion Guide designed to help program leaders consider the key ideas discussed in this chapter. These questions are designed to support you in beginning the important discussions about these key topics with other stakeholders and decision makers in your organization.

## NOTES

1. Linda Darling-Hammond, Ruth C. Wei, Aletha Andree, Nikole Richardson, and Stelios Orphanos, "Professional Learning in the Learning Profession: A Status Report on Teacher Development in the United States and Abroad." Dallas, TX: National Staff Development Council, 2009.

2. Jonah E. Rockoff, "Does Mentoring Reduce Turnover and Improve Skills of New Employees? Evidence from Teachers in New York City" (Working Paper 13868). Cambridge, MA: National Bureau of Economic Research, 2008. Accessed from: www.nber.org/papers/w13868; Pamela Grossman, Susanna Loeb, Jeannie Myung, Donald Boyd, Hamilton Lankford, and James Wyckoff, "Learning to Teach in New York City: How Teachers and Schools Jointly Determine the Implementation of a District-Wide Mentoring Program." *National Society for the Study of Education Yearbook.* New York: Teachers College, Columbia University, 2012.

3. Rockoff, "Does Mentoring Reduce Turnover and Improve Skills of New Employees?," 23–24.

4. Ibid.; Grossman, Loeb, Myung, Boyd, Lankford, and James Wyckoff, "Learning to Teach in New York City."

5. Rockoff, "Does Mentoring Reduce Turnover and Improve Skills of New Employees?"

6. Grossman, Loeb, Myung, Boyd, Lankford, and Wyckoff, "Learning to Teach in New York City."

7. Marjorie E. Wechsler, Kyra Caspary, Daniel C. Humphrey, and Kavita K. Matsko, "Examining the Effects of New Teacher Induction." Menlo Park, CA: SRI International, 2010.

8. Liam Goldrick, David Osta, Dara Barin, and Jennifer Burn, "Review of State Policies on Teacher Induction." Santa Cruz, CA: New Teacher Center, February 2012.

9. Jim Knight, "Instructional Coaching: What We Are Learning About Effective Coaching Practices." Presentation to the National Staff Development Conference, Orlando, Florida, December 6, 2008.

10. Lee S. Shulman, "Knowledge and Teaching: Foundations of the New Reform." *Harvard Educational Review* 57, no. 1 (1987): 1–23.

11. Sharon Feiman-Nemser and Michelle B. Parker, "Making Subject Matter Part of the Conversation in Learning to Teach." *Journal of Teacher Education* 41, no. 3 (1990): 32–43.

12. Steven Glazerman, Eric Isenberg, Sarah Dolfin, Martha Bleeker, Amy Johnson, Mary Grider, and Matthew Jacobus, "Impacts of Comprehensive Teacher Induction: Final Results from a Randomized Controlled Study" (Report No. PR10-74). Washington, DC: Mathematica Policy Research, June 2010. Accessed from: http://www.mathematica-mpr.com/publications/PDFs/education/teacher induction-fnlrpt.pdf.

# 5

# Using Data to Support Continuous Program Improvement

| Well Developed |
| --- |
| *Program systematically gathers quantitative and qualitative implementation data (i.e. time spent with mentor, mentoring processes used, program quality) and seeks to show direct impact on retention, teacher practice and student learning.* |
| *Data is collected from multiple sources including mentors, new teachers, principals, students, and other stakeholders.* |
| *Data is regularly shared and analyzed with mentors, stakeholders, and others to show impact and collaborate to make strategic programmatic improvements.* |

When first beginning a mentoring program, it is easy for leaders to get caught up in the challenging task of organizing the program, finding mentors, collaborating with stakeholders, and managing daily operations. With all of those tasks to manage, it is easy for leaders to underestimate the importance of developing systems of data collection and analysis from the earliest stages of program development.

In an era of school accountability and particularly in tough economic times, not having good data about an educational program can have dire consequences. This is particularly true for programs like mentoring that can often fly under the radar of those who make budgeting and staffing decisions in a school or district. In fact, program leaders often comment that collecting data that shows mentoring is working is a job requirement. If they cannot show impact, their program is likely to be shut down.

So what kind of data should a mentoring program start collecting? Or, if you are already collecting some data, how do you improve in this area? This chapter will explore three key areas:

1. types of data to collect
2. strategies for data collection
3. how to use that data both internally and externally

## TYPES OF DATA TO COLLECT

There is a great deal of data mentoring programs could choose to collect in order to effectively evaluate a program's success and to share its impact with the superintendent, board members, mentors, new teachers, and other school and community stakeholder groups. To help narrow it down, let's consider two big buckets into which programmatic data generally fall: data related to programmatic *implementation* and data related to programmatic *impact*. Implementation data is generally straightforward data that counts things, whereas impact data is more complicated to gather because it seeks to show how the program is creating an effect on others.

| Counting | Program Quality | Retention | Practice | Student Learning |
|---|---|---|---|---|
| *Who are we reaching—directly and indirectly?* | *How well is the program being implemented?* | *Are we retaining teachers over time?* | *In what specific ways is practice becoming more effective?* | *How and in what ways is student learning improving?* |

| Data of Implementation | Data of Impact |
|---|---|

New Teacher Center Impact Spectrum
(*Source*: New Teacher Center, 2011.)

Whether a program decides to gather implementation data, impact data, or both really depends on the type of question one has about the program. Let's take a look at each type of data in turn and consider the types of questions that could be addressed by such data sets.

1. *Implementation Data.* The most straightforward kind of programmatic data to collect is what some statisticians call *counting metrics*. Counting refers simply to the numbers—things we can count. For example:

a. How many mentors do we have in our program?
b. How many new teachers is our program serving?
c. How many students are being taught by new teachers?
d. How many schools have new teachers in them?

This kind of data is reasonably easy to collect, and many programs generally have easy access to it.

Another counting data has to do with time. For example:

a. What is the average length of a mentor–new teacher interaction?
b. How frequently are mentors and new teachers meeting?
c. How much time are mentors spending in professional development?

d. How much time are mentors spending driving between sites?
e. How much time are mentors spending on other duties such as paperwork completion?

Again, this is reasonably easy data to collect. Many program leaders ask mentors to complete time sheets that indicate the amount of time they are spending on various activities as part of accountability processes. These time sheets can be easily mined for this type of information. Or, more generally, this data can be collected through surveys of mentors and new teachers, perhaps at the mid and end of the year.

A slightly more sophisticated type of data to collect is *program quality metrics*. This type of data answers questions related to how the program is being implemented and at what level of quality and fidelity. Data might be collected on questions such as:

a. How are mentors and new teachers spending their time together (i.e., what mentoring processes are mentors and new teachers undertaking together)?
b. What standards are mentors and new teachers focusing on?

This kind of data can be very useful to program leaders and mentors as they work to develop norms and expectations within a group of mentors. For example, program leaders might ask mentors to gather data on what processes mentors were engaging new teachers in during their work together. After a year of collection, they might have data that looks something like this:

Table 5.1. Sample Program Data: Mentor Report of Time Spent on Mentoring Processes

| Mentor | One-to-one coaching (hours) | Teacher observation (hours) | Coteaching (hours) | Phone or email (hours) | Video conference (hours) | Other support (hours) | Total support (hours) | Total interactions | Avg. interaction length (hours) |
|---|---|---|---|---|---|---|---|---|---|
| 1 | 63.5 | 33.92 | 9.08 | 0.66 | 0 | 1.5 | 108.66 | 102 | 1.06 |
| 2 | 78.08 | 114 | 0.5 | 0.92 | 0 | 0 | 193.5 | 152 | 1.27 |
| 3 | 101.15 | 80.66 | 4.42 | 5.92 | 2.1 | 18.75 | 213 | 157.78 | 1.35 |
| 4 | 130.83 | 112.83 | 0 | 6.75 | 5.4 | 34.25 | 290.06 | 177.95 | 1.63 |
| 5 | 71.04 | 110.12 | 0 | 3.14 | 2.05 | 2.1 | 188.45 | 202.63 | .93 |
| **Total** | **444.6** | **451.53** | **14** | **17.39** | **9.55** | **56.6** | **993.67** | **792.36** | **6.24** |
| **Avg.** | **88.92** | **90.31** | **2.8** | **3.48** | **1.91** | **11.32** | **198.73** | **158.47** | **1.25** |

Another example of mentoring frequency and process data gathered from new teachers might look like this:

**Table 5.2. Sample Program Data: New Teacher Report of Mentoring Frequency and Process**

|  | Never | < Once a month | Once a month | Several times per month | Once a week | Almost daily | Combined impact |
|---|---|---|---|---|---|---|---|
| Planning during the school day | 20.0 | 8.6 | 18.1 | 17.1 | 36.2 | 0.0 | 53.3 |
| Being observed teaching by my mentor | 1.9 | 10.6 | 25.0 | 23.1 | 36.5 | 2.9 | 62.5 |
| Observing my mentor's teaching | 76.9 | 14.4 | 2.9 | 1.9 | 3.8 | 0.0 | 5.8 |
| Planning instruction with my mentor | 17.5 | 18.4 | 20.4 | 20.4 | 23.3 | 0.0 | 43.7 |
| Having discussion with my mentor about my teaching | 0.0 | 3.8 | 5.7 | 21.0 | 63.8 | 5.7 | 90.5 |
| Meeting with my mentor outside the school day | 42.9 | 21.9 | 20.0 | 9.5 | 5.7 | 0.0 | 15.2 |

This kind of data is very useful for program leaders, as it allows them to quickly see which processes mentors are using and which they are not using. It also allows them to see which mentors are spending significantly more time with new teachers and which ones are spending significantly less time with their new teachers. When program leaders see mentors who are outperforming, they can ask those mentors about strategies they are using to manage their time, for example. The data invites the program leader and the mentors to ask the right questions of themselves in a non-critical way and to explore possibilities together.

One northeastern program is gathering this data from mentors regularly for accountability as well as to support mentor growth and development. Each month, program leaders create reports for individual mentors about their time with each new teacher. Are they spending more or less time than average? Are they engaging in a range of mentoring processes? What standards are mentors and new teachers addressing? Are those appropriate for the development of the new teacher? The data allow the program leader and the mentor to engage in the conversation in a timely way.

Implementation data is a valuable starting point for gathering information about how many are being served by the program and the quality of that implementation.

2. *Impact Data.* How do you know if your mentoring program is making a difference? This question should be a catalyst for program leaders to take a deeper look at the results of the program and understand its effects on multiple stakeholders. To answer this question, a second, and more sophisticated, kind of programmatic data is needed to illustrate the impact that a mentoring program is having on retention, teacher practice, and student learning. This data can have important uses within a program, but it is also extremely valuable to share with stakeholders and others who determine whether induction programs continue to operate and their level of funding. Let's take a look at each in turn.

Probably the most easily answered impact data to gather is intended to answer the question, "Are we retaining more teachers in our school or district as a result of our program?" In many cases, the initial reason for beginning a mentoring program was to increase the retention rate of new teachers, so it is important to be able to show this impact. Connected to basic questions about whether or not the retention rate improved, more complicated inquires might also be interesting. For example:

a. How many new teachers are staying in their original school? In the district? In the profession? How long are they staying beyond their induction experience?
b. How do our retention numbers among mentored teachers compare with nonmentored teachers in our district?
c. How much did the mentoring experience impact the new teacher's decision to stay or leave the school or district?
d. How do our retention numbers among mentored teachers compare with other districts (in our local area? in our state? in our nation?) that either have or do not have mentoring programs?

Below is a sample of what retention data might look like:

Table 5.3. Sample Program Data: Yearly New Teacher Turnover

| | 1st Year | 2nd Year | 3rd Year | Summary | |
|---|---|---|---|---|---|
| | | | | Total | % of Total |
| # of New Teachers | 168 | 143 | 110 | 421 | |
| # of New Teachers Not Returning to District | 21 | 24 | 17 | 62 | 14.72 |
| % Not Returning | 12.5 | 16.78 | 15.45 | | |

This data shows how many teachers are currently in their first through third years of teaching in the district and their retention rate at the end of each year. When compared to, for example, the rate of turnover that existed in the district before mentoring was implemented or the rate of turnover for comparable districts in the area, this can be powerful data to share because it can clearly show the impact of mentoring on retention.

*Impact data focused on retention* might also be useful to gather about mentors. For example:

a. How long do mentors continue to serve in their positions (especially if there is no time limit on mentor service)?
b. What do mentors do after they complete their time as mentors? (i.e., what positions do they take postmentoring?)
c. How long do mentors remain in their school, district, and profession after serving as mentors?

Tracking this data over time and in comparison to data from other schools and districts can help program leaders make a clear case for the value added by mentoring and induction and the importance of maintaining such programs. If a leader can say, for example, that by creating an induction program in the district, teacher retention has already increased by 25 percent over the last two years, that is impressive. If the leader can further add that the retention rate of new teachers in their district is now 32 percent higher than other similar districts in their state that do not have induction programs, there is a significant chance that induction program is going to be around for a while.

It can also be useful for program leaders to use data to internally measure their own progress and success against programmatic goals and to consider possible changes to structures and processes. For example, if retention rates have risen for teachers in their first two years in your school or district, but then decline after year three, perhaps this warrants further study as to why this drop is occurring postinduction. Is there something contextually in the district that is contributing to this loss of teachers at this point in their career? Is there something, perhaps, that the induction program might do that could increase retention rates over a longer period of time? Answering these questions can further strengthen a mentoring program as well as the district's teaching force overall.

Mentoring is about more than simply retaining teachers in the field, however. It is also intended to help accelerate the practice of new teachers. Therefore, gathering data about the specific ways that new teachers' practice is becoming more effective is also a valuable source of impact data. Gathering *teacher practice impact data* is significantly trickier than counting new teachers served or even tracking retention because there are a number of factors that can impact a new teacher's practice that are not related to mentoring. These include prior teacher education experiences and readiness for mentoring, other learning experiences the new teacher is having, school climate and culture, and administrative support, among other possibilities. These mitigating factors mean the questions program leaders have to ask are, by nature, more complicated. For example, some research questions might include:

a. How are new teachers improving as a result of mentoring? How do we know?
b. Which mentoring processes seem to make the biggest difference in improving teacher practice? How do we know?
c. How are new teachers rated by their evaluators? How does this compare with the evaluations of veteran teachers?

If, for example, a program could collect data that shows that second-year teachers receiving mentoring support are using instructional practices that make them as effective as fourth-year teachers, this is useful data to share with stakeholders, mentors, and new teachers.

Data gathered from new teachers aimed at answering some of these questions might look like this:

Table 5.4. Sample Program Data: New Teacher Perceptions of Mentor Program Helpfulness

|  | No help at all | Helped a little | Helped some | Helped a lot | Help was critical |
|---|---|---|---|---|---|
| General instructional strategies | 5.8% | 2.9% | 16.3% | 53.8% | 21.2% |
| Curriculum for subject content I teach | 10.5% | 14.3% | 28.6% | 35.2% | 11.4% |
| Classroom management | 3.8% | 5.7% | 21.0% | 49.5% | 20.0% |
| School and/or district policies and procedures | 3.8% | 8.7% | 22.1% | 45.2% | 20.2% |
| Completing required new teacher processes | 1.9% | 1.0% | 8.6% | 36.2% | 52.4% |
| Completing other school or district paperwork | 2.9% | 2.9% | 18.1% | 37.1% | 39.0% |

This data could help program leaders to determine where mentors are having the most impact, as perceived by new teachers, and where they are not currently being as useful. Such data could be triangulated with other information to determine where and if changes in the mentoring program need to be implemented.

Leaders could ask questions about the impact of their program on mentor practice as well. Again, the goal here is to help new teachers by developing knowledgeable and skillful mentors who can move teacher practice forward. So knowing what mentoring practices new teachers say, for example, have the biggest impact on their practice, and there is data showing that these practices are leading to an increase in new teacher knowledge and skill, this would be great data to share with mentors.

Further, if a program is delivering professional development to mentors on a regular basis on these identified high-leverage practices, a natural question to ask might be, "How are mentors improving as a result of our program's professional development? How do we know?" Being able to show that as a direct result of a learning experience, mentors are using new strategies or skills in their work with new teachers that impact new teacher practice and, hopefully, student learning, this is valuable data. If, on the other hand, the impact is not evident, what else should the program be providing to mentors to help develop that knowledge or skills that the professional development intended?

Finally, and perhaps most challenging of all, is attempting to gather data about a program's *impact on student learning.* Answering the question, "How, if at all, is student learning improving as a result of mentoring?" is considered the Holy Grail of induction research. The research on this topic is currently not robust because of the many intervening variables between mentor support and student learning. Like the challenges data collectors face when attempting to determine the impact of mentoring on teacher practice, there are many possible reasons students may or may not show progress that may or may not be directly attributable to mentor support. Generally, according to Michael Strong, "Districts and schools that have created mentoring programs for new teachers have found that student achievement rates are up."[1] Kate Barret et al. add that for teachers of high-need students, mentoring seems to lead to particularly significant achievement gains.[2] However, this research is anecdotal at best. While student impact data may be challenging to gather, it should not stop programs from making an attempt to gather evidence indicating a correlation between mentoring and student outcomes.

Some questions programs could ask related to the impact of mentoring on student learning are:

a. How, if at all, is student learning improving as a result of mentoring? How do we know?

b. In comparison to the students of veteran teachers, how are new teachers' students achieving?

c. How are specific student populations being impacted? How do we know the impact of mentoring on them?

One piece of data collected to look at this question might be student achievement data that compares new teacher and veteran students. Such data might look like this:

Table 5.5. Sample Program Data: Comparative Test Results for New and Veteran Teachers' Students

| Geometry | All Students | | Honors Students | | New Teacher Significance | |
|---|---|---|---|---|---|---|
| | New Teachers | Veteran Teachers | New Teachers | Veteran Teachers | All Students | Honors Students |
| Achievement level average | 2.97 | 2.78 | 3.79 | 3.38 | Significantly higher | Significantly higher |
| Scale score | 40.40 | 37.69 | 56.92 | 48.05 | Significantly higher | Significantly higher |
| Number of students taught | 670 | 2598 | 53 | 217 | | |
| Number of teachers | 15 | 56 | 2 | 1 | | |

Collecting data that makes linkages between mentoring and student learning, again, makes a great case for the value of mentoring to stakeholders. After all, the goal of schools is to leverage all of their resources to increase student learning. Therefore, if a mentoring program can show connections between their work and student learning, they have literally proven their worth. Seeing the test results of new and veteran teachers' students compared side-by-side in the table above makes a good case for the potential impact of mentoring on teaching and learning. Of course, this data would need to be triangulated with data that show how mentoring specifically led to these results, but this is an important starting point.

Internally, it is a useful exercise for mentors and program leaders to attempt to make these links between mentor practice and processes and student outcomes. It can help a program to really hone in on what, specifically, seems to lead to clear changes in teacher practice that are directly reflected in student learning. Discussions with mentors about what exactly they did and examination of artifacts of student practice that are the direct result of changes in teacher practice can be extremely enlightening for all parties. Such exercises can lead to the deepening of knowledge and skill for all who participate. Again, while it is not an easy task to gather this kind of data, the implications for programmatic improvement make this a worthwhile task to take on.

## STRATEGIES FOR DATA COLLECTION

One of the biggest challenges in programmatic data collection is simply determining how to collect the data you need to answer your questions. Luckily, there are a wide range of sources program leaders might use to gather both implementation and impact data. Three common sources of information are:

1. mentors
2. others connected to or impacted by the mentoring program
3. other school or district programs with useful data

Each of these sources by themselves can provide a unique and rich perspective on the implementation and impact of the mentoring program. Skilled program leaders develop systems to regularly gather data from each of these sources in order to triangulate their findings and harness the power of the data to systematically and continuously improve the quality and impact of the program on new teacher practice and student learning.

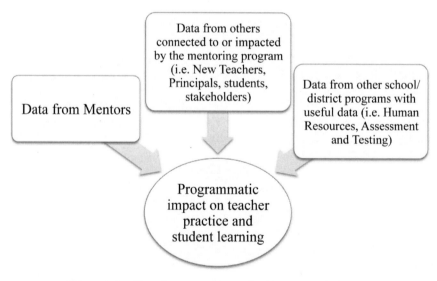

Triangulating Data Sources to Determine Programmatic Impact

### Mentors

Many mentoring programs begin by collecting data from the mentors. This is usually reasonably easy as mentors are directly within the sphere of influence of program leaders. Some programs build implementation data collection into their systems from the beginning by asking mentors to complete travel logs, time sheets, or other accountability-type data collection processes. Some programs use technology such as Google Forms, which can allow for regular data collection in real time as well as give easy access to data by program leaders for analysis purposes.

Mentors are also the easiest source of impact data. Because mentors and program leaders are often together for professional development or other meetings, they can be more easily surveyed, interviewed, and shadowed in the field to gather the quantitative (numerical) and qualitative (anecdotal) information on new teacher and student impact needed to answer more complicated impact data collection questions.

## Others Connected to or Impacted by the Mentoring Program

When mentoring programs seek to expand their data collection processes beyond their mentors, the next logical step is to gather information from those connected to the program or for whom the program in some way impacts. Generally, this includes new teachers, principals and other stakeholders and, sometimes, students. Unlike data from mentors that is easily collected as part of mentoring work, this data can be slightly more challenging to gather and cannot be gathered as often as data from mentors.

Most programs that seek input on programmatic implementation and impact from new teachers and principals do so mainly through surveys once or twice a year. For example, in the Santa Cruz/Silicon Valley New Teacher Project in California, new teachers and principals are asked to complete an online survey at both the middle and end of the year. The survey, which contains both closed-response items (i.e., answered with a Likert scale such as a scale of 1 to 5) and open-ended questions (i.e., short written response), is brief and is easily completed in less than ten minutes. Mentors encourage new teachers and principals to complete the survey within the time frame.

Programs like SC/SVNTP often ask the same questions over time in an attempt to gather longitudinal data about programmatic implementation and impact as well as to compare perceptions of the program by various groups. For example, do mentors, principals, and new teachers agree on how often mentors and new teachers are meeting? Is there general correlation between what these three stakeholder groups feel is the impact of mentoring on teaching and learning? Close analysis of this data within and across groups is useful for program leaders as they work to make continuous programmatic improvement.

In addition to surveys, some programs take data collection from new teachers, principals, and other stakeholders a step further. Some programs choose to interview a subset of people in these groups in order to gather further qualitative data. While interviewing is a time-intensive process, it can be helpful, particularly if it is used strategically to illuminate points on a survey, for example, that seemed ambiguous after looking at the quantitative data.

Data collection from students is slightly trickier, though there are some programs that are looking to use this data source to determine programmatic impact more regularly. Surveys of students about their classroom environment, their teacher and her practice, and their learning taken between one and three times over the course of the year can provide very interesting data about how a teacher's practice is changing over time and how that is impacting students. When triangulated with data from mentors, teachers, and others, this can be very useful to draw correlations between what mentors and new teachers are doing together that has a specific and measurable impact on students.

## Other School or District Programs with Useful Data

Expanding beyond those who are directly connected with the program, some mentoring programs reach out to other school or district programs that gather other useful data.

When Durham, North Carolina, decided to transition to a full-release mentoring program in their district in 2005, the program director made the strategic move to coordinate with Human Resources and the Office of Testing to gather regular data on new teachers and their students. Human Resources was able to provide data about new teacher evaluations that allowed program leaders to track improvement of new teachers over time. They could, for example, use an initial evaluation cycle as a benchmark for where a cohort was at the end of the first semester, compare this data set with the same cohort after a few evaluation cycles, and determine whether the cohort as a whole as well as individual teachers were either growing or plateauing over time.

Through a partnership with the testing office, induction program leaders were able to gather targeted data about students who were currently being taught by new teachers being supported by mentors and compare them with the performance of the students of other veteran teachers. Program leaders were pleased to find that even in the first year of the induction program, new teachers' students were often outperforming the students of veteran teachers.[3]

This story provides a valuable reminder that program leaders do not always have to invent ways to gather data on programmatic impact. Much of the data they require is probably already being gathered in the district, and all program leaders need to do is seek it out. Gathering data from multiple sources both within and external to the mentoring program about programmatic implementation and impact allows program leaders to carefully analyze the strengths and needs of the current program and to pinpoint successes and exactly where changes need to be made.

## USE OF DATA INTERNALLY AND EXTERNALLY

The value in the collection of data is, of course, in how it is used. Thoughtfully collecting data helps programs to tell the story of the program's quality and impact. But when resources are tight, it is important to remember two things about organizing a research and data collection agenda for your program. You are seeking to collect:

1. data that will drive a program's continuous improvement, and
2. data that will demonstrate a program's accountability for outcomes that are valued by the larger educational decision-making community.

Whether your program is in the beginning stages of collecting data or has developed a highly sophisticated process for gathering data from multiple sources, it is worthwhile to consider with whom the data is currently being shared and how it is being used to guide improvements in program quality and effectiveness. Many program leaders have commented that when they first began their programs, they did not know what questions needed to be asked and what data needed to be collected in order to answer those questions, but over time they realized that rich data could be used to their advantage on many fronts.

The ultimate goal in the data collection and analysis process should be to ensure that data is being shared and used both internally within the program and externally with stakeholders and other decision makers. Of course, the goal of sharing data with each of these two groups has different purposes. Let's take a look at each in turn.

As has been discussed briefly in the previous sections of this chapter, internal data collection and analysis should be undertaken to determine what is really working and why it is working. It can also be used to pinpoint what is not yet successful and what needs to change. Program leaders may choose to do this by themselves or share the collection and analysis tasks with their mentors as the program develops. In the first years of the Durham, North Carolina, mentoring program, for example, program leaders used mentors in collecting data about their interactions with new teachers and regularly shared back this implementation data holistically with the group as well as individually with each mentor in order to develop more even implementation and to highlight processes that led to increased likelihood of new teacher success.[4] Sharing data with mentors about time spent, mentoring process usage, standards addressed, and other topics can be of great benefit to mentors both as a group and individually. Being transparent with mentors about data collection as well as regularly sharing this data with mentors promotes buy-in and develops common vision and processes across the program.

When data is shared with external stakeholders, the general goal is to show the value-added impact of the program. Particularly when schools face economically tough times, being able to show that a program is working to improve outcomes for teachers and students is incredibly important. Stakeholders such as superintendents, school boards, funders, and other advisory groups need to see the return on their investment. The data collected on both implementation and impact from multiple sources can prove what the research suggests is true, that by reducing attrition and making new teachers more effective earlier in their career, investments in mentoring and induction pay off for schools.[5] Mentoring programs tend to work in mostly invisible ways in schools and districts—the immediate impact of them is not always visible. This level of semi-invisibility makes it all the more imperative that program leaders are collecting robust data and finding regular opportunities to share it with those who make decisions about funding and staffing.

## MAKING MENTORING WORK FOR YOU

Whether you are in the initial stages of setting up a mentoring program in your school or district or whether you have a program that has been in operation for a while, it is worthwhile to revisit your plan for continuous program improvement and the kind of data you are seeking in order to answer key questions about your program's implementation and impact on teaching and learning. Below are some recommendations for program leaders related to programmatic data collection:

1. Work together with stakeholders to develop a research agenda for your program. Consider both the implementation and impact questions you would want answered.
2. Consider the sources of data you have available to you both within and external to your program. What systems of data will you need to develop, and which already exist?
3. Develop a staged/tiered plan for collecting data. What is easiest to collect? What is more complicated? As your collection process and knowledge of the programs' strengths and needs develops, you can increase the reach and complexity of your data collection process.

4. Develop a time line for gathering and sharing data internally and externally in order to foster continuous program improvement as well as to report on programmatic growth and impact.

Remember, this is a process that takes time to develop. It is reasonable to roll out a data collection plan in stages. Wherever you begin, know that setting up processes to gather data in service of continuous program improvement is a worthy endeavor.

## READY TO TAKE THE NEXT STEP?

At the end of this section, there is a Discussion Guide designed to help program leaders consider the key ideas discussed in this chapter. These questions are designed to support you in beginning the important discussions about these key topics with other stakeholders and decision makers in your organization.

## NOTES

1. Michael Strong. "Does new teacher support affect student achievement," *Research Brief* #06, 1 (2006).

2. Kate Barrett, Katherine Hovde, Zehua Li Hahn, Katherina Rosquetta. High Impact Philanthropy to Improve Teaching Quality: Focus on High-Need Secondary Students. Philadelphia, PA: Center for High Impact Philanthropy at the University of Pennsylvania, 2011.

3. Fred Williams (Former Durham, North Carolina, Induction Program director), in conversation with the author, January 2014.

4. Ibid.

5. Anthony Villar and Michael Strong, "Is Mentoring Worth the Money? A Benefit-Cost Analysis and Five-Year Rate of Return of a Comprehensive Mentoring Program for Beginning Teachers." *ERS Spectrum* 25, no. 3 (2007): 1–17.

# Section I Discussion Guide

## SECTION CONCLUSION

No two mentoring programs are exactly alike, as each caters to the individual culture and specific needs of its unique school or district. They are effective because they have taken the elements described in this section and tailored them to meet the unique contextual needs of their school or district. Making mentoring work for you requires engaging in ongoing discussions with stakeholders to set programmatic priorities and guidelines and to best organize resources and support.

The following pages show a list of topics and sample questions based on the recommendations from this section that will help you build a plan of action and successfully start or improve your mentoring program. You can talk about all of them over time, or pick and choose the ones that coincide with the part of the rubric that is your program's current area of focus.

| **I. Successful induction programs carefully select, train, and utilize mentor's valuable skills and knowledge to support new teacher success.** | | |
|---|---|---|
| **Essential Question:** *How can we ensure we choose the best mentors, provide them with the training they need, and utilize their skills in the best possible way?* | | |
| **Successful Implementation** | **Questions to Consider** | **Ideas Generated for Program Development** |
| **A. Careful Selection of Mentors** | | |
| The induction program works closely with stakeholders to clearly define criteria for mentor selection, which include subject matter teaching and adult learning expertise. | Mentor Selection Criteria:<br>➤ *Who should be involved in determining criteria for mentor selection?*<br><br>➤ *What teaching knowledge, skills, aptitudes, and beliefs do we believe potential mentors should possess?*<br><br>➤ *What knowledge and experience working with adult learners do we believe potential mentors should possess?*<br><br>➤ *Will they have release time to mentor? Will that release be part- or full-time?*<br><br>➤ *How long will mentors be released from classrooms to serve as mentors?*<br><br>➤ *What other leadership opportunities will mentors be able to explore either during or after their time as mentors?* | |
| The program utilizes a rigorous selection process to seek out, recruit, and choose highly skilled and knowledgeable teachers to become mentors. | Identification of Potential Mentors:<br>➤ *How do we know who the most effective teachers are in our school/district?*<br><br>➤ *How can we enlist the support of others in helping us locate those excellent educators who would make good mentors?*<br><br>➤ *How might we entice these excellent teachers to consider mentoring?*<br><br>➤ *Do we have enough new teachers to warrant a full-release mentor program? Can we afford it?*<br><br>➤ *If we cannot have full-release mentors, how else can we combine mentoring with teaching or other coaching roles to* | |

*(continued)*

| | | |
|---|---|---|
| | ensure mentors have sufficient release time to do their jobs as mentors well?<br><br>Mentor Selection Process:<br>➤ What is our process for choosing the best possible mentors?<br><br>➤ What questions can we ask and data can we gather that will help us to choose the best possible mentors for our program?<br><br>➤ How long will mentors serve in this capacity? Will we have time limits on mentor service? What are the positives and drawbacks of this model?<br><br>➤ What will be the career trajectory of mentors once they complete their service? Can we guarantee a return to their classrooms? What other leadership roles might mentors take up afterwards? | |

| B. Increased Mentor Capacity Through Rigorous Professional Development | | |
|---|---|---|
| **Successful Implementation** | **Questions to Consider** | **Ideas Generated for Program Development** |
| Mentors participate in timely, regular, and ongoing professional development.<br><br>Mentors are provided with an intensive and structured curriculum of professional learning that is tailored to support mentor learning in key areas including adult learning theory, mentoring language and skills, and instructional coaching. | Time for Professional Learning:<br>➤ How much time are mentors spending in professional learning? How often do they meet? Is this enough?<br><br>Planning Professional Development:<br>➤ What should our mentor professional development curriculum map include? How should it be organized?<br><br>➤ How will we know that mentors are benefitting from the learning experiences we are creating? What processes might we use to measure impact?<br><br>➤ How can we create regular opportunities for group learning as well as individualized mentor learning?<br><br>➤ What topics should our mentor professional development include? When and how often should those topics be | |

*(continued)*

| | | |
|---|---|---|
| | *discussed so they are timely?* | |
| | ➤ *How will we deepen mentor knowledge and skill over time in each of these areas?* | |
| | ➤ *How will we differentiate for the variety of experience and skill levels our mentors possess?* | |
| **Mentors set goals and develop individualize growth plans to meet those goals. Mentors receive regular feedback from program leaders to support their development.** | <u>Individualizing Mentor Learning:</u><br>➤ *What opportunities can we provide that will support our mentors in continuing to learn about their specific subject matter/grade level content and pedagogical content?*<br><br>➤ *How can we support mentors in learning the content-specific coaching skills necessary to support new teachers in these subjects/grade levels?*<br><br>➤ *How will we support mentors to develop their own knowledge and skill related to topics of personal and/or professional interest?*<br><br>➤ *How will we structure regular opportunities for mentors to collaborate on these personal areas of interest and receive feedback and support from the mentoring community?*<br><br>➤ *How can we provide opportunities for mentors to share their learnings with others so that our whole community may grow from their experiences?* | |

| **C. Strategic Deployment of Mentors** | | |
|---|---|---|
| **Successful Implementation** | **Questions to Consider** | **Ideas Generated for Program Development** |
| **New teachers are consistently matched with mentors knowledgeable about how to teach their subject matter and/or grade level to all** | <u>Content-alike mentoring:</u><br>➤ *What are our criteria for matching mentors and new teachers?*<br><br>➤ *How is the content knowledge and expertise of the mentor being considered in the matching process?* | |

*(continued)*

| students. | ➤ *How might we prioritize subject-alike mentoring?* | |
|---|---|---|
| **New teachers are consistently matched with mentors knowledgeable about the school/context/ students where the new teacher is working.** | Context-alike mentoring:<br>➤ *How many new teachers are currently matched with mentors who are knowledgeable about their school/district and their students?*<br><br>➤ *How might we reorganize our program to increase the number of new teachers matched to mentors by context?*<br><br>➤ *If we cannot match new teachers by content or context, how will we determine what tradeoffs will still result in the best possible mentoring experience for our new teachers?* | |

| **D. Protected and Well-Used Mentoring Time** | | |
|---|---|---|
| **Successful Implementation** | **Questions to Consider** | **Ideas Generated for Program Development** |
| **Protected time is provided for mentors and new teachers to meet on a weekly basis for a minimum of 1.5 hours during the school day.** | Contact Time:<br>➤ *What is the minimum amount of time mentors and new teachers should have together? What must they do together during that time?*<br><br>➤ *What is an appropriate caseload for mentors? Given our requirements for minimum number of contact hours, how many new teachers could a mentor reasonably be expected to support?*<br><br>➤ *How can we educate site administrators about the importance of protected time for mentoring? What suggestions can we make about creating this time in their schedules?*<br><br>➤ *How can we support schools in planning regular protected time for mentoring interactions?* | |
| **Mentors spend the** | Intensity: | |

*(continued)*

| majority of their time with new teachers engaged in rigorous mentoring processes that will improve immediate and long-term instruction and student learning. | ➤ How are mentors currently spending time with new teachers? What percentage of their interactions are spent talking about content and content-specific pedagogy? How much is spent on other topics?<br><br>➤ How might we support mentors in developing the content-specific mentoring skills they need in order to increase the amount of time they spend discussion content and content-specific pedagogy and the rigor of those discussions? If mentors must work outside of their content areas, how can we help them develop content-specific mentoring skills for content areas in which they did not teach? | |
| New teachers are rigorously mentored for at least two years. | Duration:<br>➤ *How can we organize our program so there is enough funding to provide support for at least two years?*<br><br>➤ *How does our induction program build on pre-service teacher education work?*<br><br>➤ *How does our program connect with other professional learning happening our school/district?*<br><br>➤ *How might we enhance these connections and create a seamless pipeline of teacher learning?*<br><br>➤ How, if at all, should the first year of new teacher support be similar and different from the subsequent years? | |

| E. Using Data to Support Continuous Program Improvement | | |
|---|---|---|
| **Successful Implementation** | **Questions to Consider** | **Ideas Generated for Program Development** |
| **Program systematically gathers quantitative and qualitative implementation data (i.e. time spent with mentor, mentoring processes used,** | ➤ *What implementation data might we collect to explore topics such as time spent with the mentor, mentoring processes used, and other metrics of program quality?*<br><br>➤ *What data might we collect to explore the* | |

*(continued)*

| | | |
|---|---|---|
| program quality) and seeks to show direct impact on retention, teacher practice and student learning. | *impact of our program on teacher retention, teacher practice, and student learning?*<br><br>➢ *As we grow and develop our program, which implementation and impact data sources could we most easily begin collecting now, and how might we develop systems over time to collect other sources?* | |
| Data is collected from multiple sources including mentors, new teachers, principals, students, and other stakeholders. | ➢ *From whom/where might we collect implementation data? Would mentors, new teachers, site administrators, students, or other stakeholders provide useful information?*<br><br>➢ *From whom/where might we collect impact data? Would mentors, new teachers, site administrators, students, or other stakeholders provide useful information?* | |
| Data is regularly shared and analyzed with mentors, stakeholders, and others to show impact and collaborate to make strategic programmatic improvements. | ➢ *How will we use this data to make strategic improvements to our program?*<br><br>➢ *With whom shall we share this data and for what purposes?* | |

# Section II: Tailoring Mentoring Support

This section delves into what new teachers often bring to their new profession, their diverse needs, and how these two areas influence their sense of efficacy as well as the way they use the induction supports available to them. Readers will explore the ways in which mentoring programs can assess the strengths and needs of new teachers, tailor support to best meet those needs, and increase the likelihood of a positive and productive mentoring relationship through the creation of a flexible mentoring program.

Although induction programs, and mentoring in particular, seem to be valuable for most new teachers, it turns out that what teachers bring with them into the profession may significantly affect what they receive.

For example, in the previous chapter it was noted that time with a mentor matters. But who gets more time with a mentor? We might assume that teachers most in need of support receive the lion's share of time. But in Pam Grossman and her colleagues' study of pathways into teaching in New York City,[1] the researcher's found that teachers who entered the classroom feeling more prepared were more likely to spend more time with their mentor. Teachers in this group were also more likely to focus on instruction rather than emotional support, and they rated their mentors as more helpful.

In contrast, teachers who indicated they felt less prepared to teach at the beginning of the school year tended to spend less time with their mentors. They were more likely to use whatever time they did spend getting emotional support and learning basic instructional skills, such as classroom management, rather than working on improving their content knowledge or instructional skills.

Prior preparation in a specific area also matters. New teachers who felt better prepared to teach English learners, for example, were also more likely to spend time focusing on this issue during mentoring. It is reasonable to suspect that novice teachers may seek—and therefore receive—help in areas in which they know what to ask for.

So what does this mean for new teacher mentoring programs? Let's take a look at three ways in which programs can begin to tailor their support to match the diverse needs and strengths of new teachers:

1. How mentors can assess new teachers' preparation, perceptions of readiness, educational philosophy, prior work experiences, and personal experiences and preferences
2. How mentors and new teachers can set and work toward goals that build on new teacher's strengths
3. How mentors can use their knowledge of new teachers to tailor their support to new teacher needs

Mentors need to know what each new teacher brings to the profession and how to determine what the new teacher needs to focus on as an individual. Mentors then need to provide support that flexes to the needs, strengths, and learning styles of the new teacher. This will allow mentors to provide the support each new teacher needs to make the most of their time together and to help the new teacher grow as far and as fast as is possible in the time allotted for mentoring.

## NOTE

1. Pamela Grossman, Susanna Loeb, Jeannie Myung, Donald Boyd, Hamilton Lankford, and James Wychoff, "Learning To Teach In New York City: How Teachers And Schools Jointly Determine The Implementation Of A District-Wide Mentoring Program," National Society for the Study of Education Yearbook. New York: Teachers College, Columbia University, 2012.

# 6

# Considerations of New Teacher Needs and Experiences

| Well Developed |
| --- |
| *Mentors gather data about teachers' preparation, perceptions of readiness, educational philosophy, prior work experiences, personal experiences and preferences to plan appropriately tailored induction experiences.* |

New teachers enter the profession with a wide range of backgrounds and experiences. They enter teaching through multiple pathways, have a wide range of knowledge and skills related to teaching their content or grade level as well as teaching diverse students, and have their own beliefs about teaching and learning. As a result of these factors, they may feel more or less ready to take on their new assignments. Their sense of efficacy can dramatically impact how they feel about the mentoring support they receive once they enter the profession, how they use that support, and how far and fast they can develop with support.

Therefore, it is important for program leaders to recognize and be knowledgeable about the differences that teacher preparation, previous experiences, and personal beliefs can have on new teachers. They also need to take these differences into consideration when providing mentoring support for those new teachers. This knowledge will allow you to organize a program that can build on the strengths with which new teachers enter teaching as well as bolster their confidence and skills in areas that may need additional support.

When considering how to tailor mentoring to best meet the needs of individuals, there are four main areas for consideration:

1. preparation for teaching and perceptions of readiness
2. educational philosophy
3. prior experiences
4. personal experiences and preferences

Each of these areas is discussed below along with strategies for gathering this data. How to best use this data will be discussed in the following two chapters.

## PREPARATION FOR TEACHING
## AND PERCEPTIONS OF READINESS

Understanding the constellation of pathways that bring teachers into your school or district is important for program leaders to understand because the knowledge, background, experiences, and beliefs about teaching that new teachers from each of these programs possess upon entering the profession vary widely and greatly impact the effectiveness of mentoring on new teacher growth.

Over the last twenty years, the number of pathways into teaching has grown significantly. Teachers can now enter through the traditional route (university-based four- or five-year programs), on emergency credentials with little to no experience or coursework, and through alternative teacher certification programs such as Teach for America, Peace Corps, Teaching Fellows, Teacher Opportunity Corps, and Teacher Residency programs. The latter have taken hold particularly in urban districts such as Los Angeles, Boston, Chicago, New York City, and San Francisco in an effort to address local shortages in the supply of math, science, and special education teachers as well as teachers willing to teach in hard-to-staff schools.

In a 2007 study by Kate Walsh and Sandi Jacobs, forty-seven states claimed to have at least one alternative route, and approximately one out of every five teachers is now prepared through such pathways.[1] Their arrival and longevity has ultimately changed the way teachers are trained in these cities and has made them major players in preparing teachers alongside university-based programs.[2]

The apparent success of these alternative programs has forced traditional university-based teacher education programs to take a hard look at the way they are preparing teacher candidates and how responsive they are to the needs of the local schools. Taking a cue from some of the more successful programs, such as the Urban Teacher Residencies, some university-based teacher education programs have adjusted their course structures and curriculum to better address the needs of the local schools where many of their teacher candidates find teaching positions. For example, in districts with an increasing number of English-language learners, teacher education programs spend more time ensuring teachers are prepared to teach such students.[3]

Similarly, alternative programs are working to refine their programs to include what traditional teacher education does best—prepare new teachers who have significant content and pedagogical content knowledge. These adjustments on both sides have made the distinction between university-based teacher education programs and alternative routes less than clear-cut.[4]

To further blur the line, many universities across the country have now partnered with alternative certification programs or developed their own programs in-house and now offer both traditional and alternative routes to teacher candidates[5] in an attempt to best meet the demands of the market.

This melding of traditional and alternative programs makes the long-standing debate about whether traditional or alternative certification is "better" at creating "effective" teacher candidates null. Perhaps a better discussion today might be about what learning and experiences teacher candidates are receiving and when, regardless of program. In Donald Boyd et al.'s study of pathways into teaching in New York City, the researchers looked at five areas that a number of scholars identified as important areas of program quality:

1. program structure (i.e., when do teachers participate in certain experiences)
2. subject-specific preparation in reading and math
3. preparation in learning and child development
4. preparation to teach racially, ethnically, and linguistically diverse students
5. characteristics of field experiences (i.e., when, how long, structure)[6]

Through their study, as well as one done by Linda Darling-Hammond and her colleagues in 2002,[7] there is some evidence that suggests the most effective new teachers have:

- strong subject-matter preparation
- intensive coursework on content pedagogy and instructional strategies for meeting the needs of diverse learners
- significant understanding of and experience with classroom management
- longer, more systematic clinical experiences

These programmatic components "may produce teachers who feel better prepared, who enter and stay in teaching longer, and who are rated as more effective."

Feeling ready to teach is also an important factor in the success of mentoring interactions. Pam Grossman and her colleagues found that teachers who entered the classroom feeling more prepared—who had a background in their subject matter and felt their coursework and field experiences were extensive enough to adequately prepare them to teach that subject to diverse students—were more likely to spend more time with their mentor. Teachers in this group were also more likely to focus on instruction rather than emotional support, and they rated their mentors as more helpful.

In contrast, teachers—especially those with emergency credentials or with no previous classroom experience—indicated they felt less prepared to teach at the beginning of the school year and, surprisingly, tended to spend less time with their mentors. They were more likely to use whatever time they did spend getting emotional support and learning basic instructional skills, such as classroom management, rather than working on improving their content knowledge or instructional skills. In essence, the job of mentors in these instances becomes to backfill these missing skills instead of accelerating practice.[8]

These results are somewhat surprising because one would assume that a new teacher who was feeling less than ready to teach would jump at the opportunity to receive support from a mentor and would try to get as much time with that person as possible. One can only speculate that perhaps these teachers who reported feeling less ready to teach were also feeling overwhelmed and could barely raise their heads from their work to seek help or were too embarrassed by their own lack of success to risk reaching out for help. Instead, they made excuses for why they didn't need help or couldn't find the time to work with their mentors. Those who were feeling more ready to teach were willing to risk having a mentor in their room to provide feedback, and they may have been eager to build on their early successes.

A new teacher's level of engagement with mentoring has a direct impact on the success of the program. When new teachers are highly engaged in induction-related activities, they consistently outperform, and have students who outperform, those new teachers who do not fully engage in all aspects of mentoring.[9]

So how do we get new teachers willing to work with their mentor whether they are feeling efficacious or not? Mentoring is most useful when it is tailored to meet the individual needs of the new teacher. This means that knowing whether a new teacher has a background in the subject matter she is teaching, or whether she feels ready to teach English learners, for example, might drastically alter if and how she chooses to spend time with her mentor.

To fully understand the prior learning experiences of a new teacher, mentoring programs, schools, and districts need to reach out to their feeder schools of education and alternative certification programs to increase communication, cooperation, and learning. Such connections allow mentors and program leaders to gather important information about what new teachers have learned already as well as what their prior teaching experiences have been like so they can appropriately tailor their programs to meet the needs of new teachers.

Mentors also need to work in close partnership with school administrators to ensure new teachers hear from their principals that spending time with a mentor is important work that the principal endorses and to make sure there is dedicated time for mentoring to occur. Understanding what new teachers need and why in some cases they might be avoiding support coupled with ensuring new teachers have time and support from their school to participate in mentoring makes it more likely to occur.

## EDUCATIONAL PHILOSOPHY

Connected with teacher education are a teacher's beliefs about teaching and learning. It is important for mentors to understand what the teacher understands, believes, and values about how teaching and learning should occur, their conceptions of the role of the teacher, and their understanding about how students learn their subject matter.

For example, if a mentor understands that a new teacher places a high value on making space in her math classroom for students to share their ideas and take intellectual risks, the mentor can support the new teacher in structuring the class in ways that will honor the voices of students and develop the skills to identify and respectfully address misconceptions related to their learning of key mathematical principles when they arise.

An understanding of what the new teacher values can help the mentor to make decisions about how to balance what is important to the new teacher with what the mentor believes the new teacher needs to know and focus on. Having conversations about what is valued by both the mentor and the new teacher can also lead to the development of a deeper and more mutually respectful mentoring relationship.

It is also important to note whether these stated beliefs are being translated into classroom practice. In a number of studies of new teachers, the researchers noted that new teachers who have been through teacher education programs often know the "right" answer to questions about what they believe about whether all students can learn, for instance, or about the most effective instructional strategies for their grade level or content area.

However, for a number of reasons, these stated beliefs might not be fully enacted in practice. One reason is that there is a "know-do gap"—a gap between the new teacher's intellectual understanding of an idea and their ability to implement the idea in practice. Another is that the stated philosophy is not their actual belief. Noting these discrepancies between stated belief and actual practice, and determining the reasons for this know-do gap, can support mentors in determining how best to make mentoring work for new teachers as individuals.

Developing an understanding about how teachers' philosophy of teaching and how it is being enacted in the classroom can help a mentor to understand why a teacher approaches a situation with students in a certain way or is drawn to a particular set of instructional approaches, for example. At the end of this chapter is a list of questions a mentor may choose to ask in order to learn more about a teacher's educational philosophy. The mentor may also want to share his answers to these questions with the new teacher as well, as this can often lead to interesting conversations that deepen the mentoring relationship and build mutual trust and respect.

## PRIOR EXPERIENCES

Just as new teachers are entering the classroom through a constellation of teacher education pathways, they are also arriving in the classroom with a wide array of backgrounds and experiences. These experiences need to be understood, valued, and taken into consideration by mentors in order to best tailor support to meet the needs of the new teacher. Specifically, there are a number of situations wherein new teachers are not at the beginning stages of their professional career and, for this reason, may need a differentiated approach to mentoring. Let's look at a few specific examples.

1. *Career Switchers.* The number of teachers who are choosing to enter the profession later in life has doubled over the last twenty years. This is in part due to the rise in alternative certification programs such as Teach for America and the Urban Teacher Residency Programs that seek out professionals from diverse backgrounds and provide fast-track programs to certification that allow a candidate to teach and take courses at the same time. These programs are particularly appealing to older teacher candidates who aren't interested in being undergrads again and want to jump in to their new careers as quickly as possible.

Career switchers decide to become teachers for a long list of reasons, which often hinge around their desire to give back to their community or to find a profession that will allow them to make a positive difference in the lives of others. Many bring deep academic and practical knowledge in math and science to their positions, which can be a tremendous asset to a school or department.

While career-switchers bring a great deal of knowledge and real-world know-how to their new roles, career switchers often find the transition to teaching even more difficult than their younger counterparts. Many come from successful careers where they spent ten or more years building knowledge, skills, and expertise in their field. They are often used to being very good at what they do and can find themselves dismayed when teaching doesn't come naturally at first. Making the switch to teaching means starting over at the bottom of the career ladder with a lot to learn. For example, while they often have a great deal of content knowledge, they've never worked with elementary or secondary-age students.

When working with career switchers, here are a few strategies for mentoring success:

- See the teacher as an equal and strive to develop a collegial working relationship.
- Find out what their goals and strengths are and use these as a basis for your interactions.
- Keep adult learning theory in mind and work to make each interaction with the teacher relevant and useful for the teacher.
- Discuss learning theory and effective techniques for teaching content to students.
- Discuss the importance of developing a positive classroom environment and effective techniques for building a classroom community.
- Provide emotional support for the teacher during the challenging transition to the classroom.
- In some cases, the new teacher might be older than the mentor. Support mentors in becoming "generationally savvy" in their interactions. Jennifer Abram's work is very helpful on this subject.[10]

2. *Emergency Credential Holders.* Each year, thousands of new teachers enter the profession with emergency credentials. Often, these teachers are hired late in the summer or after the school year has already begun to fill a vacancy that a school or district could not fill with a fully credentialed teacher. More often than not, these vacancies occur in hard-to-staff schools serving our nations' most needy children

and in subjects that are already hard to find qualified teachers for, such as math, science, and special education. While emergency credentialed teachers are well meaning and often very eager to learn to teach, most of them enter the classroom with no previous teacher education or classroom experience.

Generally, mentoring is intended to serve as a bridge from teacher education to independent teaching—to support them during the move from student of teaching to teacher of students. However, teachers on emergency credentials have nothing from which to build that bridge. They are starting from scratch.

It is important to recognize that emergency credential teachers enter teaching because they are excited about working with children or adolescents and come with a wide range of knowledge, skills, and background experiences that can be tremendous assets for learning to teach. It also needs to be understood that these teachers are starting far behind the curve and may require a very different kind of support to help them get up to speed.

For mentors who work with emergency credential holders, it is important to find out as much as possible about this new teacher's previous experiences, whether they are currently (or have ever) taken any education classes, their strengths and areas for growth, and then tailor a program specifically to meet their needs. Mentors may find they need to be more directive or instructive in their approaches and need to be ready to provide clear examples, be willing to model and coteach, and help new teachers to visit and observe other veteran colleagues to support them in developing a clear image of what high-quality instruction requires. Instead of assuming a teacher has a basic understanding of classroom management and instructional planning, for example, the mentor will need to carefully observe and provide appropriate support to begin building this new teacher's repertoire as quickly as possible.

When working with emergency credential holders, here are a few strategies for mentoring success:

- Connect with the teacher as early as possible after their hire date.
- Provide direct assistance related to immediate areas of need such as planning, pedagogy, organization, time management, classroom management, paperwork, and school procedures at the beginning of the year to ensure a positive start.
- Observe regularly and provide assistance and instruction on any areas of difficulty that present themselves.
- Find regular opportunities to model or co-observe high-quality teaching to help the teacher develop a framework for success.

- Provide emotional support for the teacher during the challenging transition to the classroom.

3. *Teachers with multiple years of experience.* There are a number of reasons why a teacher may not have received mentoring support in their first years. Some teachers enter the profession as substitutes or temporary teachers; others have been in private schools or districts that did not offer mentoring or could not offer mentoring support to all new teachers. Regardless of the reason, you may find yourself working with teachers who have already been in the classroom for three or more years and now need induction support to clear their credential or for other reasons.

Seasoned teachers like these are in a very different place than the average new teacher. They have survived the transition into teaching, often with little or no support, and have begun to solidify their beliefs and practices as educators. Mentors often assume that because these seasoned teachers have been teaching for a while that they will need less support. However, because they have made this transition to teaching without support, they may have developed practices that are not ideal. This might actually mean they will need more support because the mentor must help the teacher recognize the habit and undo it before helping them to construct new instructional habits in their place.

For mentors working with veterans, the challenge is to connect as colleagues and to find a way to make the mentoring work as meaningful and useful as possible. In the previous section, we discussed how important it is for mentors to understand adult learning theory as they interact with new teachers. This is especially true for seasoned veteran teachers. The work needs to be timely, relevant, and focused on the areas of interest to them. Suggestions need to be grounded in clear reasoning and need to be doable. They are less likely to take risks or to "play" with their practice because they have already discovered their own teaching persona. If the work is about "jumping through a hoop" or completing a requirement, they will quickly find reasons to avoid mentoring interactions.

When working with teachers who already have teaching experience, here are a few strategies for mentoring success:

- See the teacher as an equal and strive to develop a collegial working relationship.
- Find out what their goals and strengths are and use these as a basis for your interactions. Do not assume more years in the classroom equates to better practice.

- Keep adult learning theory in mind and work to make each inter-action with the teacher relevant and useful for the teacher.
- Use data collection tools such as video to help the teacher con-cretely see and learn about his own practice instead of relying on the observations of the mentor.
- Make sure all suggestions are grounded in evidence, have clear purposes for their selection, and are fully described.
- Give special attention to communication: active listening, reflec-tion, and more.

Teachers entering the field through each of these unique situations do so with significant strengths upon which mentors can build an individu-alized professional development plan that will best meet the needs of the new teacher. In order to do so, however, the mentor needs to gather as much information as possible about the new teacher, their knowledge and experiences both in their previous careers and in relation to educa-tion, and their preferred work styles. At the end of this chapter, there is a questionnaire that mentors can use to gather some of this important information about the new teacher.

## PERSONAL EXPERIENCES AND PREFERENCES

While prior training and experience play a significant role in the way a new teacher begins her career and how she interacts with her mentor, her personal background, learning style, and communication style can also impact the way a new teacher perceives the mentoring experience and her willingness to work with her mentor.

Just as we expect teachers to learn about their students, their lives, their interests, and their experiences, mentors may find that learning about their new teacher's lives, interests, and experiences can be beneficial to the development of a strong mentoring relationship. While many mentors and new teachers find they can develop an effective working relationship that is purely professional—one in which the mentor and teacher talk only about their work and not about their personal lives—knowing about a teachers' lived experience can help a mentor to appropriately approach certain topics with the new teacher or to tailor their examples in ways that will be of interest to the new teacher.

In addition to understanding the life experience of a new teacher, it's also important to discuss preferences related to communication and working re-lationships. For example, it is useful to know whether a new teacher prefers to have feedback that is couched in a lot of supportive language, or whether he prefers a more straightforward, "brutally honest" approach.

It is also useful to know how and when to communicate with a new teacher. In today's technologically oriented world, many new teachers no longer prefer to talk on the phone, or even to communicate by email. Many mentors in the last few years have begun to report that their new teachers preferred text messaging as their main way of communication between meetings and requested using cloud storage systems like Dropbox or Google Drive to store documents in progress so they could have continual access to them instead of emailing. These preferences related to communication are important to discuss upfront because they can dramatically impact how mentoring occurs, when it takes place, and the new teacher's perceptions of support from the mentor. Mentors who are willing to flex their ways of communicating to meet the needs of the new teacher will find their new teachers to be more responsive and receptive than those who stick only to their preferred methodologies and schedules.

The questionnaire at the end of this chapter includes questions related to new teachers' personal context and communication styles that a mentor may choose to ask in order to ensure mentoring works well for both the new teacher and the mentor.

## MAKING MENTORING WORK FOR YOU

Successful mentoring programs take into consideration new teacher's preparation, perceptions of readiness, educational philosophy, prior experiences, personal experiences, and preferences. Learning about the experiences and priorities of new teachers can help mentors identify areas of strength and effectively build on areas of need that will best support the development of the new teacher as an individual.

Below is a questionnaire a mentor might use to gather information about the new teacher's background and experiences that would be helpful in tailoring mentoring to meet the needs of the new teacher.

A note of caution: While learning about what new teachers bring to mentoring is an important endeavor, it is important to encourage mentors to use this questionnaire in a judicious fashion. Just planting the questions in front of a new teacher and asking her to respond could easily feel like an interrogation, which is, of course, not the intent. Instead, encourage mentors to pose the questions incrementally and nonsequentially over a series of meetings as they seem relevant in an effort to better understand the background, strengths, and motivations of the teachers served by a mentor. Programs might also choose to use some pieces of this questionnaire as a screening tool that will allow the program leaders to connect new teachers with mentors whose knowledge and experiences are a good match.

---

**Pre-Service**
*Educational background, training, experiences with students, perceptions of readiness*

---

1. What is your background in the subject you are teaching this year?

2. What teacher education program did you attend?

3. What credential did you earn?

4. Have you done student teaching or worked in schools or classrooms before? What was your experience like? (e.g. what was the context? Was it similar or different in comparison to your current placement?)

5. Have you worked with this specific population before? (e.g. culturally, ethnically, and/or linguistically diverse students?)

6. Did you complete a Teacher Performance Assessment as part of your program? (What were your thoughts about that experience? What did you think about the scores? Was it an accurate assessment of your practice? What did you learn from that experience?)

7. How are you feeling about teaching this year?

---

**Practices in Pedagogy**
*Experience with the components of effective classroom instruction*

---

1. What is your personal philosophy of teaching?

2. How do children/adolescents learn (your subject)?

3. What motivates (this age group of) students to learn (your subject)?

4. What prevents students from learning (your subject)?

5. What makes learning (this subject) stick?

6. What do teachers need to know about students?

7. How should we assess learning (of this content or for students at this grade level)?

8. How should we keep track of learning from individuals and groups (in this content or at this grade level)?

---

Learning About New Teacher Strengths, Needs, and Experiences Questionnaire

9.  What role do student language and culture play in learning?

10. What is the best environment in which to learn (your subject matter)?

11. What are the responsibilities of the teacher and the student (at this grade level)?

## Philosophy of Teaching
*Beliefs about teaching and learning, content instruction, and the role of teacher and student*

1.  What is your personal philosophy of teaching?

2.  How do children/adolescents learn (your subject)?

3.  What motivates (this age group of) students to learn (your subject)?

4.  What prevents students from learning (your subject)?

5.  What makes learning (this subject) stick?

6.  What do teachers need to know about students?

7.  How should we assess learning (of this content or for students at this grade level)?

8.  How should we keep track of learning from individuals and groups (in this content or at this grade level)?

9.  What role do student language and culture play in learning?

10. What is the best environment in which to learn (your subject matter)?

11. What are the responsibilities of the teacher and the student (at this grade level)?

## Educational and Work Background
*Strengths and insights gained from previous work experiences*

1.  Why did you decide to become a teacher?

2.  Tell me about some of the work experiences you have had prior to becoming a teacher. What did you find rewarding? What was challenging about them?

3.  How long have you been teaching? What was your previous teaching context like?

4.  What did you learn from your prior work/teaching experiences that you are finding useful as you begin this teaching position? What have you found those experiences did not prepare you for?

Learning About New Teacher Strengths, Needs, and Experiences Questionnaire
*(continued)*

| **Communication Styles and Preferences** |
| :---: |
| *Logistics for communicating, planning meetings, sharing resources, providing feedback and information* |
| 1.  What is the best way to communicate with you? |
| 2.  What are the best times for us to meet or to talk? What times are off limits? |
| 3.  What is your level of comfort with feedback (1 "need lots of support" → 5 "brutally honest")? |
| 4.  What is your level of comfort with technology for communication and collaboration? |

| **Personal Context** |
| :---: |
| *Personal interests, home and community background, values* |
| 1.  What are some things you enjoy doing outside of work? What are your interests and talents? |
| 2.  How do you maintain a work/life balance? |
| 3.  What would you like me to know about your family, culture, values, or beliefs? |

Learning About New Teacher Strengths, Needs, and Experiences Questionnaire

## READY TO TAKE THE NEXT STEP?

At the end of this section, there is a Discussion Guide designed to help program leaders consider the key ideas discussed in this chapter. These questions are designed to support you in beginning the important discussions about these key topics with other stakeholders and decision makers in your organization.

## NOTES

1. Kate Walsh and Sandi Jacobs, *Alternative Certification Isn't Alternative.* Washington, DC: Thomas B. Fordham Institute, 2007.

2. Pamela Grossman and Morva McDonald, "Back to the Future: Directions for Research in Teaching and Teacher Education." *American Educational Research Journal* 45, no. 1 (2008): 184–205.

3. Tamara Lucas and Jamie Grinberg, "Responding to the Linguistic Reality of Mainstream Classrooms: Preparing All Teachers to Teach English Language Learners." *Handbook of Research on Teacher Education: Enduring Questions in Changing Contexts* 3 (2008): 606–36.

4. Kenneth M. Zeichner and Hilary G. Conklin, "Teacher Education Programs." In *Studying Teacher Education: The Report of the AERA Panel on Research and Teacher Education*, edited by Marilyn Cochran-Smith and Kenneth M. Zeichner. Washington, DC, 2005.

5. Kate Walsh and Sandi Jacobs, *Alternative Certification Isn't Alternative*.

6. Donald J. Boyd, Pam Grossman, Hamilton Lankford, Susanna Loeb, and Jim Wyckoff, "How Changes in Entry Requirements Alter the Teacher Workforce and Affect Student Achievement." *Education Finance and Policy* 1, no. 2 (2006): 176–216.

7. Linda Darling-Hammond, Ruth Chung, and Fred Frelow, "Variation in Teacher Preparation: How Well Do Different Pathways Prepare Teachers to Teach?" *Journal of Teacher Education* 53, no. 4 (2002): 286–302.

8. Pamela Grossman, Susanna Loeb, Jeannie Myung, Donald Boyd, Hamilton Lankford, and James Wyckoff, "Learning to Teach in New York City: How Teachers and Schools Jointly Determine the Implementation of a District-Wide Mentoring Program." *National Society for the Study of Education Yearbook*. New York: Teachers College, Columbia University, 2012.

9. Marnie Thompson, Pamela Paek, Laura Goe, and Eva Ponte, "Study of the California Formative Assessment and Support System for Teachers: Report 3, Relationship of BTSA/CFASSTand Student Achievement (CFASST Rep. No. 3, ETS RR-04-32)." Princeton, NJ: Educational Testing Service, 2004.

10. Jennifer Abrams and Valerie von Frank, The Multigenerational Workplace: Communicate, Collaborate, and Create Community. Thousand Oaks, CA: Corwin, 2014.

# 7

# Planning for New Teacher Growth and Development

| Well Developed |
| --- |
| *Mentors and new teachers regularly work together to co-assess new teachers' strengths and needs against a set of professional teaching standards and to set meaningful goals aligned with new teacher needs and interests.* |
| *Mentors and new teachers plan a rigorous course of work that supports new teachers in making progress towards those goals.* |

As mentioned previously, teaching is incredibly complex work and learning to do it well as quickly as possible takes a deliberate approach. It is sometimes hard, as a mentor, to know how to strike the right balance between helping new teachers with their immediate needs (i.e., classroom management, problem solving about students, planning for tomorrow) and with long-term needs (developing a sustainable way to plan at the unit and course level, expanding understanding of appropriate ways to teach a particular content to students, developing reflective habits).

To help strike this balance and ensure that mentors succeed in pushing the development of new teachers as far and as fast as possible in the limited amount of time mentors have to work with new teachers, it is valuable for mentors and new teachers to develop a road map for their work together.

Teachers learn best when there are clear standards of practice and when they are actively engaged in their own learning. It would be easy for mentors, who are often selected because they are stellar teachers with a track record of success in the classroom, to feel that "they know best" and dictate where new teachers should focus. However, this approach does not breed success. As adult learners, new teachers need to feel that they have some control over what they do and how their learning happens.

As Lee Shulman explained,

Authentic and enduring learning occurs when the teacher is an active agent in the process—not passive, nor an audience, not a client or a collector. Teacher learning becomes more active through experimentation and inquiry, as well as through writing, dialogue, and questioning. Thus, the school settings in which teachers work must provide them with the opportunities and support for becoming active investigators of their own teaching.[1]

Instead of taking over, mentors need to see themselves as partners in the work. While it is important to recognize that mentors have significant knowledge and skill to share with new teachers and should, therefore, have input about what a new teacher needs and where that new teacher should focus their attention, mentors also need to keep at the heart of their work a respect for the knowledge and skills of all teachers; a dedication to treating teachers as partners and adult learners; and a focus on identifying teachers' assets and building on their strengths. In a well-structured mentoring program, trained mentors regularly engage in professional conversations with new teachers about their practice that guide new teachers in a meaningful process of self-assessment, goal setting, and regular review/reflection on their progress toward these goals. Mentors also support new teachers in creating a rigorous plan of action that will help new teachers to develop these habits of mind for themselves as well as helping them to grow as far and as fast as possible in the brief time they receive mentoring support.

Since the early 1980s, there have been numerous studies indicating that goal setting leads to increased productivity and self-confidence in numerous professions and circumstances. In education, Patricia Ashton, Alfred Bandura, and Jacquelynne Eccles and Allan Wigfield's work is widely cited for their findings that when teachers self-assess their performance, set goals, and analyze their work against those goals, their "personal teaching efficacy"—the beliefs teachers have in themselves as effective teachers—is increased. Further, this efficacy influenced by goal attainment is a significant predictor of teacher practice and student outcomes.[2]

Engaging new teachers in meaningful professional learning requires the mentor and new teacher to develop a common language or framework for understanding what good teaching looks like and what good teachers do. Using a set of research-based standards can help to create this common language, illuminate the new teacher's areas of strength and need, and can serve as a basis for these important conversations. Such frameworks can also help mentors and new teachers to plan a progression of work because they provide a rubric or progression from novice to expert around each standard.

In order to strike the appropriate balance between short- and long-term learning needs of the new teacher, mentors and new teachers benefit from engaging in planned experiences that support new teacher growth and development.

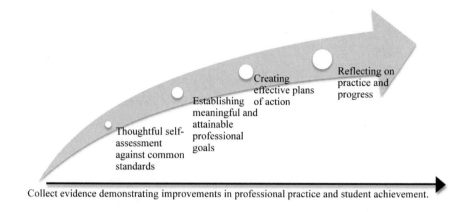

Creating
effective plans
of action

Reflecting on
practice and
progress

Establishing
meaningful and
attainable
professional
goals

Thoughtful self-
assessment
against common
standards

Collect evidence demonstrating improvements in professional practice and student achievement.

Planning for New Teacher Growth and Development

As the graphic above indicates, there are four key components of effective mentoring for new teacher growth and development:

1. thoughtful self-assessment against common standards
2. establishing meaningful and attainable professional goals
3. creating effective plans of action
4. reflecting on practice and progress

Throughout the process, mentors and new teachers work together to collect data that documents improvement. Let's look at each of these areas in more detail.

## THOUGHTFUL SELF-ASSESSMENT AGAINST COMMON STANDARDS

The first component of the teacher development process involves new teachers taking stock of their current practice with support from their mentors. In order to do this, however, it is valuable for mentoring programs to first define what they believe good teaching entails.

There are many organizations that have clearly delineated what good teaching looks like in the form of standards. Many have also created tools for self-, peer-, or evaluator analysis against these standards as well as tools for observing the components of effective teaching in action. Many schools, districts, and states have developed their own standards that define effective teaching practice. Here are a few examples:

- The state of California has created the California Standards for the Teaching Profession (CSTP) that provides a narrative overview of what is expected of professional educators in the state and includes six domains and thirty-nine elements. The accompanying Continuum of Teaching Practice (CTP) provides a breakdown of each of those elements into rubric form showing the progression of experience from novice (emerging) to expert (innovating).[3]
- The Council of Chief State School Officers (CCSSO), through its Interstate Teacher Assessment and Support Consortium (InTASC), developed a set of research-based, model, core teaching standards. The stated goal of these standards is to "outline what teachers should know and be able to do to ensure every K–12 student reaches the goal of being ready to enter college or the workforce in today's world."[4] The InTASC standards are grouped into four general categories and ten standards. Each standard is described in terms of teacher performance, essential knowledge, and critical dispositions.
- Charlotte Danielson's *Framework for Teaching* includes four research-based domains of teaching divided into twenty-two elements and further into subelements that seek to define and describe teaching. Rubrics are provided for each element along with further descriptors. There are numerous tools and templates that can be used to observe and assess using these components.[5]
- The University of Virginia's Classroom Assessment Scoring System (CLASS) defines good teaching where there is interaction between teacher and student. The tool breaks down practice into three large domains and further into elements developed through extensive research and field testing. Each element has a carefully delineated rubric with narrative descriptions of practice at each level. CLASS has even created a subscription-based video library where teachers can see multiple examples of each element and learn about strategies for improving practice related to that element. There are also variations of the CLASS instrument that can be used depending on the grade level of the class.[6]

Whether a school or district decides to create its own set of standards for excellent teaching or use a set created by a district/charter organization, state, national professional organization, or outside organization, the intention is the same—to create a common vision of excellence in teaching and to provide a common language to describe what teachers should know and be able to do in order to achieve that level of excellence.

In mentoring programs, standards play a particularly important role in that they define for both the mentor and the new teacher what the school, district, state, and/or profession believe teachers should seek to develop in themselves and their practice. Because national and state standards reflect visions of good teaching, they can shape conversations about instruction and learning. When mentors help new teachers assess their current practice and progress against standards, they induct new teachers into professional habits of inquiry and norms of accountability.

While standards are integral to the work of mentoring, they also offer some challenges for new teachers and mentors. The language of many state and national standards is what one mentor in Sharon Feiman-Nemser and her colleague's new teacher induction study called "a thick foreign language book" that has to be interpreted before beginning teachers can integrate them into their teaching instead of treating standards and teaching as separate tasks.[7]

Similar to the way teachers use standards in classrooms to guide the development of curriculum and learning experiences for students, the role of the mentor is to support new teachers in working through this thick language to understand what good teaching looks like, to seamlessly integrate the standards into their ongoing work with new teachers in a way that meets both their immediate and long-term developmental needs, and to help new teachers to achieve the expectations of the standards as a logical part of their instructional work.

For example, a new teacher struggling with managing student behavior can, with the support of a mentor, see what constitutes an unsatisfactory teacher response to student misbehavior as well as what the progression from unsatisfactory to basic to proficient to exemplary might look like.

Unlike principals or other evaluators, mentors bring a nonjudgmental point of view to these discussions and, therefore, new teachers are able to reflect honestly, without fear of reprisal about their current level of performance in relationship to a standard. Then, under the guidance of a mentor, the new teacher can explore the current instructional decisions and their impact as well as the possible implications of making different decisions. Then she can work with her mentor to improve her skill in this area with a clear, standards-based trajectory in mind.

In order to assess new teachers against standards, mentors and new teachers need to gather data about the new teacher's current level of practice in relationship to the previously described standards of professional practice. This data might be anecdotal—teacher description of their practice currently or during their student teaching experience—or observational—mentor-collected evidence of current practice, or it might be collected evidence of students' current level of practice.

Using this data, the mentor and new teacher can work together to coassess current practice against the standards. Coassessment ensures that the new teacher is taking an honest look at his or her own practice. Coassessment, as opposed to self-assessment, means that the mentor and new teacher look at the practice of the new teacher together using data and evidence as the foundation for their decisions. The mentor brings a more experienced set of eyes to the discussion and can support new teachers in neither being too hard nor too easy on themselves as well as helping to further define and name the practices that accompany each of the standards. Coassessment supports the teacher to acknowledge and build on strengths while, at the same time, pushing for improvement.

## ESTABLISHING MEANINGFUL AND ATTAINABLE PROFESSIONAL GOALS

In order to support the new teacher in making progress against standards, it is important that the teacher feel the work he or she is undertaking is meaningful and worthy of their time and will support the teacher in mastering the set of professional skills and abilities that lead to student achievement. Setting meaningful and attainable professional goals that build on their current level of practice on professional standards is a good step in that direction.

As most professional teaching standards have a large number of elements, it is best if mentoring programs pair down the standards to a small number that, when focused on by new teachers and mentors, will have the most dramatic impact on teacher learning and student success. For example, the California Standards for the Teaching Profession contain six domains and thirty-six elements. Asking new teachers to set goals on all, or even most of those standards, would be an overwhelming and useless task. Instead, choosing a small subset of discreet elements allows mentors and new teachers to focus more deeply on what is most important in the first years of teaching without feeling the process is overkill.

From this paired-down list of standards, mentors can work with new teachers to select a few key standards on which they'd like to focus more deeply and work with the new teacher to codevelop professional goals in relation to those standards. Most people can only focus on a very small set of goals at a time productively. Therefore, mentors would be wise to help new teachers focus on developing only two to three discrete goals at a time.

When developing goals, some mentoring organizations like to use SMART goal language. SMART goals have the following characteristics:

S    Specific and Strategic
M    Measurable
A    Attainable and Action Oriented
R    Rigorous, Realistic, and Results Focused
T    Timed and Tracked

## S = Specific and Strategic

Goals need to be straightforward and clearly written. They need to be specific enough to determine whether or not they have been achieved. A goal is strategic when it serves a clear purpose in advancing teacher learning and is likely to have a positive impact on student growth.

## M = Measurable

If we can't measure it, we can't manage it. Mentors might support new teachers in asking questions such as, "What measures of quantity, quality, and/or impact will we use to determine the goals have been achieved?" "What information will we use to measure progress?" and "How will we measure progress over the course of this inquiry?" Throughout the process of working toward the goal, the mentor and new teacher will need to periodically check in and ask the question, "Are we doing what we said we were going to do?"

## A = Attainable and Action Oriented

Goals should have active, not passive verbs, and the action steps attached to them should tell us who is doing what. Mentors need to ask the question, "What will you do to achieve your goal?" Without clarity about what we're actually going to do to achieve the goal, a goal is only a hope with little chance of being achieved. Mentors and new teachers need to work together to lie out a plan that will make clear the actions required to achieve their goal. This kind of planning helps new teachers to feel confident that they can tackle this goal, stay focused and energized, and persist even when there is a lot going on in their daily professional lives.

## R = Rigorous, Realistic, and Results Focused

Unlike an activity, a goal makes clear what will be different as a result of its achievement. Mentors should ask questions like, "What results do you expect?" and "How will this be measured?" A goal needs to describe a realistic, yet ambitious, result that is doable for a teacher within a reasonable period of time. Goals should stretch the new teacher, but not be out of reach, and the focus and effort required to achieve a rigorous but realistic goal should be challenging, but not exhausting. Goals set too high will discourage the new teacher from persisting, while goals set too low will leave new teachers feeling "empty" when they are accomplished and won't serve our students well.

## T = Timed and Tracked

New teachers are often busier than most new professionals and, because they often have not yet developed good systems for managing all that they must do as educators, it is easy for their own professional learning to be deemed a low priority that can easily fall off their plates. For this reason and many others, it is best if a goal has a clear deadline as well as internal deadlines when key actions will be completed and benchmarks achieved. As goals are being developed, mentors should ask: "How will we know if we are on track to accomplish our goals/have accomplished our goals?"

An addition to the SMART goal framework suggested by Doug Fisher is *interesting and relevant*. Especially when working with adults, goals need to be interesting to them and relevant to the work they are doing. If they are not, adults might nod along with their mentor as they develop their goals, but they will not dedicate the time and energy necessary to really make progress toward them.[8]

Throughout the process, mentors also need to create regular opportunities to check in about progress toward those goals by asking, "Are we where we thought we would be at this point? If not, what are we going to do to get back on track?"

Here are a few examples of SMART + I/R goals new teachers might develop:

- For each unit during the fall, I will consistently use the gradual-release model in my planning and instruction to shift learning responsibility from teacher to student.
- In order to build mastery of science content for my sixth-grade students, I will work to consistently identify and teach symbols, key terms, and other domain-specific words and phrases, using specific pedagogical techniques and additional resources to ensure comprehension.
- During the 2013 to 2014 school year, I will provide students at least two opportunities to demonstrate their learning through the use of oral presentations. Students will be provided with a rubric for presentation skills aligned to the Common Core State Standards.
- Through the implementation of a comprehensive, academic vocabulary curriculum, students in my music classes will build a conversational repertoire of musical terminology appropriate to their age level.

Each of these goals is narrow in time and scope and relevant to the teacher's current work. Progress toward these goals can also be easily measured by the teacher and the mentor. Mentors and new teachers get into trouble when they create goals that are too broad in time or scope. For example: "How might instruction on close reading, small group instruction, peer editing, and use of technology for writing support my fourth-period English students in improving their use of evidence in their writing as evidenced by the formative and summative drafts of their end-of-unit paper?"

This goal is problematic because it includes a long list of interventions. While each of these instructional strategies might, in fact, contribute to improving students' use of evidence in their writing, it would be hard for the new teacher and the mentor to analyze the impact of each of these strategies on students' work. Instead, choosing one to two strategies and gathering careful data about those strategies makes it easier to see the potential impact of those strategies on student learning.

It is important to remember that setting goals at the beginning of the year is not enough. The intention of developing goals is to drive practice forward. This means that every meeting with new teachers should include a discussion of the teacher's goals and how those goals are informing and shaping their work with their mentor. This is the only way to truly make those goals live and be of use.

Also, goals are not intended to be permanent. Instead, they are intended to serve as markers of progress along the path of teacher development. Once they have been achieved, it is important to acknowledge that achievement and then set new goals. This means that, periodically, mentors and new teachers need to review and revise their goals. Research and experience suggests taking the time to revisit goals every four to six months to determine whether they are still the right ones on which to focus is an important endeavor. This time frame is long enough to allow the new teacher to make significant progress toward their goals so there is a sense of fulfillment, but also short enough that mentors and new teachers can sustainably focus on them without the momentum of progress being diminished. Most mentoring programs suggest setting professional goals in late fall, revisiting and revising in the winter, and revisiting them again at the end of the school year. However, as previously mentioned, if these goals are not brought out as a driving factor in every mentoring conversation, progress toward these goals will be haphazard at best.

Whether your program chooses to use the SMART goal model or another strategy, the intention in writing goals is to provide a framework that will guide collaboration between a mentor and a new teacher for a few months in ways that focus both on new teachers' and students' immediate needs as well as on their long-term learning needs. Setting goals that are meaningful for teachers support what they need now and in the future. Remember, as with all parts of highly successful mentoring programs, we want new teachers to see this process of goal setting as useful to their work and as a process they will continue to undertake long after their mentors are out of the picture. In order to do so, the work needs to feel sustainable and meaningful.

## CREATING EFFECTIVE PLANS OF ACTION

Setting goals are an important part of the process to intentionally move new teachers' practice forward, but goals without clear plans of action to accomplish them are not useful.

One approach to action planning that many mentoring programs have used with great success is to develop cycles of inquiry. It is defined as "a process through which teachers study their own practice in order to change and strengthen their teaching."[9] Also called action research (see chapter 5 for a description of action research), the goal of this process is to support teachers in becoming "active investigators of their own teaching" through self-assessment, reflection on practice, and professional conversation. Through inquiry, teachers can become empowered to comprehend, confront, and address challenges they face in their classroom. Mentors support new teachers in developing this effective habit of practice by scaffolding and guiding new teachers through the inquiry cycle, helping new teachers to collect data on student learning, serving as thinking partners, observing and gathering data on teaching practice, and fostering reflection on the process.

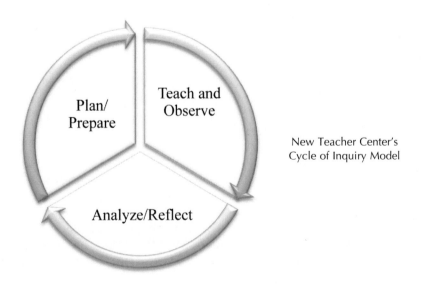

Plan/ Prepare

Teach and Observe

Analyze/Reflect

New Teacher Center's
Cycle of Inquiry Model

Effective new teacher inquiry action plans are defined in different ways by different organizations. The New Teacher Center uses the three-step model of: 1) plan/prepare, 2) teach and observe, and 3) analyze and reflect.

The National School Reform Faculty defines the cycle of inquiry as a five-step model of: 1) analyze data, 2) frame or reframe key issues or questions, 3) investigate literature and field expertise, 4) develop and tune the action plan (goal, strategies, data collection to measure success), and 5) carry out strategies and collect data.[10]

These are just two of many models teaching organizations use to define the cycle of inquiry. Across all the various models, there are some common elements that are important for any mentoring program to include in their new teacher action plans:

1. collect and analyze data
2. frame important questions of practice
3. research and planning
4. apply learning and collect data
5. analyze data again

Let's walk through each of these components and consider how mentors can support new teachers at each stage.

### Collect and Analyze Data

Mentors can start by helping new teachers to gather data about student learning needs and strengths as well as other data about students (i.e., the language needs, special learning needs, learning styles, interests). Then, mentors can support new teachers in taking a close look at student data both as a whole group and as individuals who have specific needs and abilities. Mentors can also help new teachers to notice patterns that emerge from the data and consider how those patterns might help to identify what students need at this particular moment, such as a new instructional delivery model or a change in the learning environment.

An important note about data: Student data is a broad category that can include both quantitative and qualitative measures and can be from both formative and summative sources. Possible data sources might include a paragraph written in class, notes taken during an observation of a small-group interaction, an exit ticket, or an end-of-unit assessment. Each of these sources provides a window into student thinking and current levels of proficiency and, therefore, are important sources of information for teachers. New teachers need support from their mentors in learning how to develop a regular habit of analyzing a wide range of student data sources for trends and using the information from that analysis to plan effective and differentiated lessons that meet the needs of the students in their classes.

## Frame Important Questions of Practice

From this close look at the data, mentors can help new teachers to frame a question they have about their practice and/or about student learning. Mentors and new teachers can consider questions such as, "What do we want to know more about from looking at the data? How does this intersect with my professional goals?" Mentors want to frame inquiry questions in similar ways to goals. As mentioned previously, they should represent small and manageable inquiries that are doable within a short period of time and which will provide some clear evidence of their impact on the teacher's practice as well as on student learning. Mentors and program leaders may want to develop sentence frames to guide the development of inquiry questions that are SMART + I/R aligned. For example, "How might _____ improve my ____ students' ability to _____ as evidenced by _____?" Such a frame supports both mentors and new teachers in creating clear, specific, and measurable goals that are aligned with new teacher work and interests.

## Research and Planning

Almost all inquiry questions require new teachers to try on new ways of being with students that are outside of their current repertoire of practice. This means they will need to do some learning in order to be prepared to answer their question. Most new teachers don't know where to find information about how to improve their practice, which provides mentors an opportunity to help new teachers learn how to research, connect, and plan.

This stage of the inquiry process is a great opportunity for mentors to help new teachers connect with other veteran educators who might be trying strategies new teachers are interested in learning and to take them to visit those teachers in their classrooms. It is also a great opportunity to help new teachers connect with professional organizations where they can find resources and other colleagues beyond their school who have similar interests. Both of these opportunities not only help the new teacher answer their questions and move their practice forward, they also help new teachers to deepen their collegial connections and build support systems that will sustain them after their period of mentor support ends.

## Apply Learning and Collect Data

Once mentors and new teachers have gathered data about possible strategies for answering the inquiry question, the mentor and new teacher can work together to create a lesson or sequence of lessons that support the development of students' knowledge and skill in relation to the specified area of need using their new information. This is an opportunity for mentors to gauge new teacher's skills with planning and to provide models and support that will help new teachers develop healthy and sustainable planning habits.

Then, new teachers have the chance to try out strategies and implement the lesson plans codeveloped with their mentor. Mentors can support during this stage by continuing to remind new teachers about their goals and objectives, reviewing lesson plans and asking questions, role-playing, modeling, coteaching, and engaging in cycles of observation wherein they observe and gather data about what is being implemented, look through that data with the new teacher, and provide feedback about practice.

## Analyze Data Again

Finally, mentors and new teachers can gather and review data again and consider how the teacher and student benefitted from engaging in the inquiry process and consider next steps. This process of going again to the data further solidifies the value of the data in teacher's practice as well as the understanding that nothing is ever really summative in teaching—it is always a continuous cycle of inquiry.

The cycle of inquiry described here appears to be a linear process. In actual implementation, however, teachers and mentors can enter the cycle at any point, and they often move back and forth between steps. It is also valuable for new teachers to understand that this process does not have to be an arduous and lengthy one that lasts for a semester and ends with a formal twenty-page paper. While some inquiries may stretch out over a period of weeks or months, many can occur in the course of a week. The goal is that when new teachers complete their induction phase, they have incorporated this process into their regular way of working and are doing something like this, however informal, on a regular basis. Again, the intention is to support new teachers in developing a very effective habit of constantly questioning their practice and adjusting based on data. This process supports new teachers in building their own sense of control and efficacy in the classroom. We want them to think, "There is always something that I can do to better support student learning, and I know how to go about making that happen."

## REFLECTING ON PRACTICE AND PROGRESS

A reflective approach to work is an important habit of mind we want all teachers to cultivate. Reflection means that new teachers take the time to deliberately assess their practice and consider what worked and didn't work and consider what to do next time to improve their practice as well as to enhance learning experiences for all students.

Therefore, throughout the process of growing teacher practice, mentors should seek to question beginning teachers in ways that promote self-assessment and reflection. Below is a sampling of questions mentors might choose to ask in order to foster a reflective stance:

- What worked? What are one or two specific things you did that led to success?
- What do you feel was less than successful? Why?
- To what degree do you think your lesson met your learning objective(s)?
- What did students get from the experience? For whom was this lesson most successful? Which students did not benefit as much?
- If you had a chance to teach this lesson again to the same group of students, what would you do differently?
- How might you support your students in moving forward in your next lesson(s)?
- Did you depart from your plan? If so, how and why? How, if at all, did the modification improve the lesson?
- How might collaboration with other colleagues, resource personnel, and/or families support student learning?

What is important is that teachers think clearly about their practice and focus their thinking on student learning. Asking questions such as these provides new teachers the space and time to think deliberately about their practice and consider alternative perspectives. Given the prompt, "If you had a chance to teach this lesson again to the same group of students, what would you do differently?" a new teacher might respond, "Well, now that you mention it, I don't think the directions for the activity were clear; I'd better revise them before I do this lesson again" or, "I discovered that I should never put those two students together! They didn't concentrate on their work." Making space in a busy day for new teachers to reflect in this way helps them to develop the internal process of asking themselves these questions so that the practice of regular reflection will become engrained and will persist long after the mentor is no longer there to facilitate the process.

Just as a note, you may have noticed that, intentionally, none of the example questions listed above begins with the word *why*. *Why* questions tend to elicit defensive responses on the part of the new teacher and, therefore, are to be avoided in order to maintain the reflective and open stance that mentoring is intended to create.

Beginning teachers are not the only ones to benefit from well-designed and well-executed plans for new teacher growth and development. The mentors themselves find value in focusing their attention on teaching practices that promote high levels of student learning, and they often reconsider their own practice in the course of working with their beginning teachers. In fact, many mentors report that their own teaching has improved as a result of working with new teachers on their inquiries.

## MAKING MENTORING WORK FOR YOU

Supporting new teachers in accelerating their growth and development under the guidance of a trained mentor is at the heart of a strong mentoring program. Such an important process should not be left to chance. In the face of all the demands that new teachers must manage each day in their practice, it is easy for their own learning to get lost. Strong mentoring programs provide structures that help mentors and new teachers to build effective plans for new teacher growth and development by:

- *creating a standards-based program.* Create or locate a set of professional teaching standards that work well for your context and clearly define those standards so that a new teacher and mentor can coassess against those standards. Ensure that the number of standards against which new teachers are responsible for assessing their practice is manageable.
- *delineating a process for mentors and new teachers to codevelop and regularly revisit meaningful goals.* Mentors and new teachers need to have the time and space to think about the long-term learning of the new teacher. Develop processes and time lines through which mentors and new teachers work together to create SMART + I/R goals that are of value to the new teacher and will create meaningful growth both for the new teacher and his or her students.
- *developing a process through which mentors and new teachers create doable plans of action tailored to the needs and strengths of each new teacher.* Support mentors by creating structures that can scaffold

inquiry-based experiences for new teachers wherein new teachers develop effective ongoing learning and problem-solving habits, understand how to use data effectively, develop strategies for finding and using information about best practices, and engender a reflective habit of mind.

Programs that develop these support structures for ongoing new teacher learning as well as support mentors in learning how to gracefully and strategically use these processes will see big gains from their new teachers. These gains exist not only during the period when new teachers are being mentored but also last long into their professional careers.

## READY TO TAKE THE NEXT STEP?

At the end of this section, there is a Discussion Guide designed to help program leaders consider the key ideas discussed in this chapter. These questions are designed to support you in beginning the important discussions about these key topics with other stakeholders and decision makers in your organization.

## NOTES

1. Lee S. Shulman, *The Wisdom of Practice: Essays on Teaching, Learning, and Learning to Teach*. San Francisco: Jossey-Bass, 2004, 513–14.

2. Patricia Ashton, "Teacher Efficacy: A Motivational Paradigm for Effective Teacher Education." *Journal of Teacher Education* 35, no. 5 (1984): 28–32; Alfred Bandura, "Social Cognitive Theory: An Agentic Perspective." *Annual Review of Psychology* 52 (2001): 1–26; Jacquelynne S. Eccles and Allan Wigfield, "Motivational Beliefs, Values, and Goals." *Annual Review of Psychology* 53, no. 1 (2002): 109–32.

3. Commission on Teacher Credentialing, "California Standards for the Teaching Profession (CSTP)." Sacramento, CA: 2009.

4. Council of Chief State School Officers Interstate Teacher Assessment and Support Consortium (InTASC) Model Core Teaching Standards: A Resource for State Dialogue. Washington, DC: Author, 2011, April. Accessed from: http://www.ccsso.org/Resources/Programs/Interstate_Teacher_Assessment_Consortium_(InTASC).html.

5. Charlotte Danielson, *Enhancing Professional Practice: A Framework for Teaching*. Alexandria, VA: ASCD, 2007.

6. Classroom Assessment Scoring System (CLASS). Charlottesville, VA: Teachstone. Accessed from: http://www.teachstone.com/about-the-class/.

7. Sharon Feiman-Nemser, Cynthia L. Carver, Daniel S. Katz, and Sharon Schwille, *New Teacher Induction: Programs, Policies, Practices.* Final Report. East Lansing, MI, 1999.

8. Doug Fisher, "Close Reading of Complex Texts." Presentation to the Santa Cruz/Silicon Valley New Teacher Project and the Santa Clara County Office of Education. San Jose, California, January 25, 2014.

9. Tom Malarkey, "Inquiry for Equity: What Does It Mean for Teacher Research?" In *Working toward Equity*, edited by Linda Friedrich, Carol Tateishi, Tom Malarkey, Elizabeth R. Simons, and Marty Williams, 11–21. Berkeley, CA: National Writing Project, 2006.

10. National School Reform Faculty (2014). Cycle of Inquiry. www.nsrf harmony.org.

# 8

# Tailoring Mentoring Programs to Appropriately Support New Teachers

**Well Developed**

*Mentors understand their role is to tailor mentoring to best fit each new teacher's assessed needs and context in order to ensure the rapid growth and development of each new teacher.*

*Mentors know how to use a set of flexible processes to guide their interactions with new teachers, gather data on classroom practice and student learning, foster reflection, and provide accountability.*

As has been described in a previous section, all new teachers enter the profession with different levels of experience and with widely varied knowledge, strengths, needs, and interests. They may have had rich preservice or early career experiences that have well prepared them for teaching and primed them to be receptive to mentoring support, or they may be arriving with little prior experience and knowledge and feel overwhelmed with all there is to know and master in order to even get through a day with students.

They also enter different contexts wherein the culture of the school and the needs of the students are widely varied. Therefore, in addition to learning general content and pedagogical practices, new teachers need to learn situationally relevant approaches to teaching. They need to know how to teach their subject to students in ways that will help the students in front of them get it; they need to think on their feet; they need to analyze situations as they come and decide what to do; they need to study the effects of their practice; and they need to know how to use what they learn to inform their planning and teaching.[1]

Despite this diversity of teacher need and instructional contexts, many mentoring programs continue to provide a single-track or generic approach to mentoring. Such programs require all new teachers—regardless of experience, need, readiness, or context—to complete the same processes and go through the same experiences in the same order to ensure that all new teachers are consistently exposed to important practices, habits, and learning opportunities. When mentoring programs take this approach, they do a tremendous disservice to new teacher learning and, consequently, to the future of those new teachers and to student learning because they are not taking the unique needs of the teacher and context into consideration.

To ensure new teachers have the most useful experience while working with their mentor, leaders need to create a program that:

1. provides individualized, personalized, and contextualized mentoring for new teachers
2. ensures mentors understand that their role is to tailor mentoring to best fit each new teacher's assessed needs and context in order to ensure the rapid growth and development of each new teacher
3. supports mentors in developing and using a set of flexible tools and processes to guide their interactions with new teachers, gather data on classroom practice and student learning, foster reflection, and provide accountability
4. holds mentors and new teachers accountable for the learning of both the new teacher and the students

Let's take a look at how each of these components support the development of a mentoring program that is responsive to the unique needs of each new teacher and his or her students.

## PROVIDE INDIVIDUALIZED, PERSONALIZED, AND CONTEXTUALIZED MENTORING FOR NEW TEACHERS

It is very easy for program leaders and other stakeholders to assume that all new teachers entering a school or district would have the same prior knowledge and need the same things and, therefore, should have the same set of experiences during their induction. However, as has been discussed in a previous section, this assumption is extremely faulty. Teachers enter with a wide range of prior experiences and knowledge and are placed in contexts with students that have specific needs. Creating a single-track program will not meet the needs of all teachers (in fact, it will meet the needs of very few teachers) and can lead to significant dissatisfaction from both teachers and mentors because they will feel the program duplicates what they received in their preservice program or is otherwise not a meaningful use of their precious time. Teachers in such programs often refer to them as a bunch of hoops to be jumped through and boxes to be checked off instead of an authentic program that meets their needs.

Let's take, for example, the three case study teachers introduced at the beginning of this book and consider how a mentor might consider their experiences and needs and design an appropriate mentoring experience for each of them.

*Diane is a first-year high school chemistry teacher in an urban district. She has an undergraduate degree in biology and, as a part of her teacher residency program she was an intern teacher in a biology classroom. She generally feels well prepared to teach biology—but not chemistry. In addition, she has found that her alternative urban school differs dramatically from the suburban school where she did her student teaching.*

Diane has strong science content knowledge and attended a teacher education program that provided her with science-specific pedagogy as well as a student teaching experience. What she mainly needs is support in making the transition from biology to chemistry and support in understanding the context of her new school setting. Diane needs a mentor who has a strong chemistry background to help her gain both the content and pedagogical content knowledge she needs to be successful in her content area. She also needs explicit support from her mentor in learning about her alternative education students—What are their strengths and needs? How can Diane adapt her instructional strategies to best support their learning?

*Jerome has recently accepted a kindergarten position at the elementary school where he student taught during his university teacher preparation program. Having previously taught in this school as a teacher candidate means he knows many of the teachers in the school and has a strong support network. However, during his student teaching, he worked only in third- and fourth-grade classes, which leaves him feeling unprepared to work with students this young. He is struggling to figure out how to handle the developmental needs of four- and five-year-olds and how to deal with anxious parents.*

Jerome is entering the profession with strong contextual knowledge of the school and its community. He probably already has a network of colleagues with whom he can work and knows the norms for working in this school. He also has a strong knowledge of elementary content and pedagogy from his teacher preparation program and student teaching experiences. Jerome may not necessarily need a mentor who is knowledgeable about his context as a result. What he does need is a mentor who has kindergarten-specific knowledge and can help him to adapt the knowledge and skills he already possesses to meet the needs of his young students. He also needs support in effectively developing the skills and processes to regularly communicate and collaborate with parents.

*Tamako spent the last ten years working in the business world and has recently decided to make a career change. She has accepted a position as a middle school math teacher on an emergency credential and is taking classes at night toward a teaching degree. She has a great deal of real-world knowledge to bring to her role, but having never student taught, she has little experience with classroom management, curriculum development, and the needs of young adolescents.*

This new teacher brings with her a strong mathematical background and a wealth of experiences from the business world that can help her show her middle school students the true value of math in the world. However, her lack of preparation and experience in schools means she needs a mentor who can quickly help her to develop classroom management routines, get to know her students and how they learn, and understand how to plan units and lessons by breaking down mathematics into learnable chunks and sequences for middle schoolers. Also, because she is a career switcher, Tamako needs a mentor who understands how to effectively build a relationship and communicate with someone who is not in their twenties.

Each of these new teachers comes with strengths and experiences upon which mentors can be built. They also all need different things that are specific to their context, content, and prior experiences. However, asking all of them to attend, for example, extensive professional development sessions on lesson planning may not be the best option. While Tamako might find these sessions to be incredibly useful, they are not what Jerome or Diane need most. Creating a flexible program that pairs each of these new teachers with a skillful mentor who can assess their strengths and needs and design individualized, contextualized, and personalized learning experiences to support them in meeting their goals is a more effective approach.

Instead of creating a single-track curriculum for all new teachers, mentoring programs that work provide a clear vision of the professional standards, habits of mind, and/or other outcomes they want to see new teachers develop. Then, they train and task mentors with the important job of assessing each new teacher's developmental and contextual needs and creating a personalized and responsive approach that will best support the new teacher in reaching those outcomes.

Creating an individualized, personalized, and contextualized approach means a program will need to keep five things in mind:

1. *Flexible mentoring programs are practical and relevant to the assessed needs and context of the teacher.* Mentors need to know how to learn about the prior experiences of a new teacher and their knowledge and skills in relation to professional standards. They also need to have a working knowledge of the school, its student population, and other contextual needs that can impact new teacher success. Mentors need to continually work at the nexus of teacher needs and contextual demands to support teachers in gaining the practical knowledge and skills they need to be successful in this specific situation.

2. *Flexible mentoring programs are developed with consideration of the other demands placed on their time.* There is a tremendous press of time on teachers. There are only so many hours during which teachers can teach, plan, evaluate student work, meet with students, collaborate with others, and still have time to eat, sleep, and have a life outside of school. Mentors need to make sure that each time they meet with a new teacher it is a worthwhile encounter and that new teachers leave the meeting with what they need to improve their knowledge and practice in both the short and long term. While this book does suggest programs should set flexible parameters around how much time new teachers and mentors should spend together, mentors should be able to work within those parameters to best meet the scheduling and learning needs of each teacher as an individual. For example, instead of meeting for an hour and a half each week, perhaps it is more useful to meet with the new teacher for an hour on Mondays with a thirty-minute follow-up on Thursday.

3. *Flexible mentoring programs are aligned with the needs and the school or district in which the new teacher is working.* Mentors need to learn about the priorities of the school and/or district in which the teacher works and work with school and/or district administrators to ensure that what they are focusing on with their new teacher is in alignment with what the school wants and needs them to focus on. Creating this kind of alignment of goals and educational philosophies ensures that the mentoring experience is not an add-on program separate from the daily needs of the teacher but, instead, is an integral part of their daily experience.

   For example, if a mentor and a first-year teacher decide to develop a goal focused on increasing differentiation in the classroom, but the teacher's assistant principal has instructed the new teacher to focus on classroom management, then the mentoring program is out of alignment with the school. In this situation, the job of the mentor should be to help the new teacher see the latter as a more appropriate goal for their first year and help the new teacher to meet that goal.

4. *Flexible mentoring programs build on and deepen the new teacher's content knowledge, pedagogical skills, and their ability to effectively teach content to students.* Teachers work at the intersection of content and students. This means teachers need to not only know their subject matter well, they also need to know how to effectively teach that subject matter to their specific students. Mentors need to be knowledgeable about both the new teacher's content and effective pedagogical strategies for teaching that particular content. They also need to know what the new teacher learned during their preservice or other prior teaching experiences about both content and pedagogy so as not to duplicate those experiences but, instead, to build on and deepen that initial learning.

Programs also need to have plans in place for teachers who enter a school or system with significant prior experience and who are already high-quality teachers but, perhaps, still need induction support. For example, some programs have an early completion option for teachers who move into their district with significant prior experience and a record of high-quality teaching already. Candidates for this program are selected based on mentor's standards-based observations and letters of recommendation from previous/current administrators. Such teachers engage in a shorter program wherein the mentor and teacher work together to support the teacher in learning primarily about the school and students. A similar option also exists in some programs for teachers earning a second certification after they have already earned a cleared credential in another subject or grade band. Mentors work with new teachers for a shorter period of time to support them in learning the new knowledge and skills necessary for this new context.

5. *Flexible mentoring programs balance what new teachers need to know now and what they need long term.* One of the most challenging things about learning to teach is developing systems and processes for addressing the myriad of situations and decisions that teachers face each day. Mentors often find that they must learn to balance supporting teachers in problem-solving challenges facing them in the moment (i.e., "What do I do about this kid's behavior?" and "How do I input grades into this system?") and helping them to think long term (i.e., "What do I want my students to understand, know, and be able to do at the end of this semester?" and "How do I develop a professional community beyond my school site?"). If mentors are not careful, dealing with the crisis of the day can always take over mentoring conversations, especially for new teachers who feel less prepared to teach. There are moments when mentors need to address the crisis of the day with a new teacher; however, mentors

also need to know how to also use those moments as jumping-off points for setting up longer-term procedures and routines or when to put them aside for the moment in the interest of growing teacher practice over the long term (i.e., "Let's talk about that issue for a few minutes, then I really want to make sure we have time to look at this student work together so we can use the student data to plan your upcoming unit.").

Taken together, these five areas can create a framework for a personalized and flexible program that meets both the needs of the new teacher as an individual as well as aligning the program with the contextual needs of the school or district in which the new teacher works.

## ENSURE MENTORS UNDERSTAND THAT THEIR ROLE IS TO TAILOR MENTORING TO BEST FIT EACH NEW TEACHER'S ASSESSED NEEDS AND CONTEXT IN ORDER TO ENSURE THE RAPID GROWTH AND DEVELOPMENT OF EACH NEW TEACHER

When programs train mentors to work in a flexible system such as is described here, it is particularly important that leaders clearly articulate the purpose of mentoring. In flexible mentoring programs, the role of the mentor is to assess new teacher needs against rigorous professional standards and to design personalized learning experiences that are individually and contextually appropriate to support each new teacher to growing from where they are toward those standards of practice as quickly as possible. This means that mentors need to know how to do three things:

1. *Identify the needs, assets, and interests of each teacher with whom they work.* Mentors need to see teachers as individuals who come to the profession with unique strengths, needs, and experiences. Mentors need to know how to gather this kind of data and work with the new teacher to plan a path that will meet this teacher's individual needs. This ability to authentically assess a new teacher against the standards and plan a path right for that teacher is a skill set that mentors will need to learn from program leaders during training.
2. *Understand the context in which the teacher is working and the students with whom they work.* Many mentors are paired with new teachers at a particular school site, which makes them privy to all the contextual

knowledge a new teacher at that site would need to know. Other mentors, however, are paired with new teachers based on other criteria such as content area, which means mentors often work across multiple sites. Mentors who work in school sites unfamiliar to them need to figure out how to learn about the context in which a new teacher is working. For example, "Who do we ask when we need someone to translate at a parent-teacher conference?" or "What is the procedure for referring a student for special services?" Mentors will need training and strategies to help them learn to navigate and quickly learn about new contexts in order to best support their new teachers.

Program leaders can also help their mentors to see each other as a team whose expertise they can draw on to fill gaps in their content and context knowledge. Find opportunities to help mentors connect with each other in person at mentor meetings or electronically so they can ask questions such as, "Who would you recommend I take my new teacher to observe at the high school who has solid group work happening in their classroom?" "Which Assistant Principal should I talk to about getting a new computer for my new teacher?" or "How do we go about getting resources for science labs at this school?" Helping mentors to see each other as a team can help to ameliorate any lack of experience or knowledge of context that might exist.

3. *Have the freedom to figure out where to focus their attention with new teachers as individuals in order to best support new teachers' speedy development toward professional standards in a way that aligns with the needs and vision of the school or district.* Flexible mentoring programs need to ensure that they have hired excellent mentors and then honor the professional knowledge and skill of those mentors by allowing them to create a path that best fits the strengths, needs, and context of each new teacher. This means that mentoring programs need to make sure mentors are clear about their role and their goal in working with new teachers and have learned the mentoring language, skills, and strategies they need to do this work well.

In order to support mentors in their important and challenging work, mentoring programs need to help mentors know the key areas of knowledge and skills new teachers need to possess and how to help new teachers develop in these areas. Mentors also need to be taught how to work in a flexible manner based on what they understand about the needs and strengths of the new teacher. Finally, mentors need to be trusted to make the choices that are in the best interest of their new teachers.

## SUPPORT MENTORS IN DEVELOPING AND USING A SET OF FLEXIBLE TOOLS AND PROCESSES TO GUIDE THEIR INTERACTIONS WITH NEW TEACHERS, GATHER DATA ON CLASSROOM PRACTICE AND STUDENT LEARNING, FOSTER REFLECTION, AND PROVIDE ACCOUNTABILITY

While it is important to support mentors to make decisions about how to appropriately tailor mentoring for new teachers to meet professional and school/district standards (see previous section on goal setting), mentors need support in how to best spend their time with new teachers. While flexible mentoring programs do not necessarily specify what each new teacher should focus on in their work with their mentor (i.e., classroom management or learning a specific instructional strategy), they should provide mentors with a toolkit of protocols and processes from which mentors can select to help structure conversations and learning experiences with each new teacher to achieve these goals. Here are some examples of flexible processes from which mentors could choose:

1. goal setting against standards and action plan creation (see previous section)
2. learning about context (students, resources, and school procedures/policies)
3. communication and collaboration with colleagues and communities
4. analysis of student work to guide further instruction
5. effective lesson planning, both short and long term
6. classroom observation and data-collection processes as well as processes for providing feedback
7. problem solving
8. reflection on teacher and student learning and growth

There are a few organizations, such as the New Teacher Center, that have developed packages of flexible mentoring tools that address these areas that are worth considering. Other schools and districts have created their own sets that best reflect their specific needs, goals, and context.

Whatever your program chooses to use, the goal is to create a toolkit that will allow mentors to use their assessed knowledge of the teacher and context to create an individualized, personalized, and contextualized path toward both the program's and the teacher's individual goals.

A note of caution about mentor toolkits: The goal of creating or adapting a set of flexible tools, processes, and protocols is to help mentors have high-quality mentoring conversations about teaching and learning. They are supposed to help mentors to structure their interactions in ways that are most likely to lead to the uptake of new ideas and practices in new teachers' classrooms and to help the new teacher to develop effective habits of mind about teaching and learning. What we do *not* want is the completion of the tool to become the focus instead of the rich conversation.

This can happen very easily, especially with new mentors who are learning about the processes and developing an understanding of the complex task of mentoring. Picking a set of tools that are to be completed in a specific sequence and making sure each box on each of those tools is filled in can seem like an easier task than thinking about what a new teacher needs and having good conversations about those topics and then documenting them on the appropriate tool. Even the most well-intentioned and flexible mentoring program can become a set of paperwork to complete when the mentors misuse the tools in this way.

Therefore, it is imperative that program leaders carefully explain and teach these processes with the understanding that they are ways to structure, support, and document good conversations with new teachers, but they are not the conversations themselves. Program leaders also need to remind mentors about this on a regular basis, as it is very easy for even the most experienced mentor to slide back into this stance, especially during the busiest parts of the year.

## HOLD MENTORS AND NEW TEACHERS ACCOUNTABLE FOR THE LEARNING OF BOTH THE TEACHER AND THE STUDENTS

Providing flexible support tailored to meet the needs of each new teacher does not mean that there are no clear outcomes or goals. Mentoring programs are still responsible for ensuring new teachers are making rapid progress toward professional standards and other programmatic, school, or district goals for teachers, and that students are also making progress. To achieve this, mentoring programs that work create regular opportunities for new teachers to share their work with others and to receive feedback on that work.

In the Santa Cruz/Silicon Valley New Teacher Project (SC/SVNTP) in California, for example, new teachers turn in a portfolio twice each year that is read and commented on by other mentors in the project. The portfolio contains evidence that new teachers are applying the California Standards for the Teaching Profession (CSTP) in their classroom and are engaging in inquiry cycles with their mentors that are aligned with their CSTP goals and with the needs of their students.

As part of this process, new teachers and their mentors are given feedback on their work in relation to the standards and the programmatic expectations of the SC/SVNTP. This process holds both the mentor and the new teacher accountable for using the time they spend together in ways that are advancing the practice of the new teacher against a set of professional standards and that are leading to gains in student learning. New teachers turn in four such portfolios over the course of their two years in the project.

These portfolios not only support the new teacher in growing their practice, they also give mentors an opportunity to talk about best practices, assess their own work, and gain new ideas and strategies for best supporting new teachers. They also hold mentors and new teachers accountable for producing evidence of new teacher and student growth as a result of their work together twice each year. Program leaders use the portfolios as a source of data about what mentors and new teachers are focusing on in their work and the strategies mentors are using. This data can help program leaders to adjust the program to better meet the needs of the mentors and new teachers whom their program serves.

Assessment allows flexible mentoring programs to gather regular data about whether they are appropriately tailoring their work to best meet the needs of individual new teachers, their students, and their schools. This data provides feedback to the program, the mentors, and the new teachers in ways that allow them to further hone their work so that they are always current and viable. It also ensures new teachers and mentors are held accountable for using their time together to move new teacher and student learning forward as quickly as possible.

## MAKING MENTORING WORK FOR YOU

New teachers enter the profession with varied knowledge and experience and enter classrooms and schools that are just as diverse. A one-size-fits-all mentoring program that forces each new teacher through the same set of canned learning experiences will not provide new teachers with the kind of support they need to survive and thrive in their first years. The incredible value of mentoring is that new teachers are partnered with a one-to-one professional developer who can work with them to determine what they need and can craft learning experiences that will be meaningful and transformative for that new teacher. Successful mentoring programs, therefore, will want to keep the following items in mind in order to make mentoring work for you:

1. Create a program that values each teacher as an individual with diverse experiences and strengths. Work to ensure the program provides individualized, personalized, and contextualized support for each new teacher.

2. Educate mentors about the goals of mentoring so they are clear about their urgency and importance of their role: to work with each new teacher to learn about their strengths and needs and to tailor their work to quickly grow new teachers as far as they can in the time they are together.
3. Create or adopt a set of flexible tools/protocols to guide mentoring work. Ensure mentors understand these are protocols to guide high-quality mentoring conversation—not forms to be filled in.
4. Honor the professional knowledge and skill of mentors by allowing them to choose from among these tools/protocols in order to tailor their support to best fit the strengths, needs, and context of each new teacher.
5. Create accountability for new teacher and student growth by setting regular times to assess new teachers' work.

Programs that take this flexible stance toward mentoring will give their new teachers a richer, more rigorous, and more purposeful experience that quickly grows new teachers toward excellence than a single-track mentoring program could.

## READY TO TAKE THE NEXT STEP?

At the end of this section, there is a Discussion Guide designed to help program leaders consider the key ideas discussed in this chapter. These questions are designed to support you in beginning the important discussions about these key topics with other stakeholders and decision makers in your organization.

## NOTE

1. Deborah L. Ball and David K. Cohen, "Developing Practice, Developing Practitioners: Toward a Practice-Based Theory of Professional Education." In *Teaching as the Learning Profession: Handbook of Policy and Practice*, edited by Gary Sykes and Linda Darling-Hammond, 3–32. San Francisco: Jossey Bass, 1999.

# Section II Discussion Guide

## SECTION CONCLUSION

No two successful mentoring programs are exactly the same. They are effective because they have taken the elements described in this section and tailored them to meet the unique contextual needs of their school or district. Making mentoring work for you requires engaging in ongoing discussions with stakeholders to set programmatic priorities and guidelines and to best organize resources and support.

The following pages show a list of topics and sample questions based on the recommendations from this section that will help you build a plan of action and successfully start or improve your mentoring program. You can talk about all of them over time or pick and choose the ones that coincide with the part of the rubric that is your program's current area of focus.

**II. Successful mentoring programs tailor support to match the diverse needs and strengths of new teachers.**

| Successful Implementation | Questions to Consider | Ideas Generated for Program Development |
|---|---|---|
| **A. Consideration of new teacher needs and experiences** | | |
| Mentors gather data about teacher's preparation, perceptions of readiness, educational philosophy, prior work experiences, personal experiences and preferences to plan appropriately tailored induction experiences. | Gather data about the strengths, needs, and experiences of new teachers: <br> ➤ *How can we learn about/ support mentors in learning about each new teachers' prior experiences, personal context and communication styles?* <br><br> ➤ *How can we use this information/support mentors in using this information to appropriately tailor induction experiences for our new teachers?* | |
| **B. Goal Setting to Match New Teacher Needs** | | |
| Successful Implementation | Questions to Consider | Ideas Generated for Program Development |
| Mentors and new teachers regularly work together to co-assess new teacher's strengths and needs against a set of standards, set goals. | Create a standards-based program: <br> ➤ *What professional teaching standards should we use as the basis for our mentoring program?* <br><br> ➤ *What is a reasonable number of standards we should expect new teachers to focus on? Which ones should we choose? What are our criteria for selecting those standards?* <br><br> Create meaningful goals for new teachers: <br> ➤ *What will be the process for new teachers and mentors to set meaningful goals based on standards? Will we ask new teachers and mentors to develop SMART goals, for example?* <br><br> ➤ *How often will mentors and new teachers set/revisit goals?* <br><br> Create doable plans of action tailored to the needs and strengths of each new teacher: <br> ➤ *What instructional habits or habits of* | |
| Mentors and new teachers plan a rigorous | | |

(continued)

| | | |
|---|---|---|
| **course of work that supports new teachers in making progress towards those goals** | *mind (i.e. using data to plan instruction, reflection, etc.) do we want new teachers do develop through their work with mentors?*<br><br>➤ *What structures will we create to scaffold inquiry-based experiences for new teachers that will lead to the development of these instructional habits/habits of mind?*<br><br>➤ *How will we support mentors in learning how to effectively lead new teachers through this process?* | |

| **C. Flexible Mentoring Processes to Meet New Teacher Needs** | | |
|---|---|---|
| **Successful Implementation** | **Questions to Consider** | **Ideas Generated for Program Development** |
| **Mentors understand their role is to tailor mentoring to best fit each new teacher's assessed needs and context in order to ensure the rapid growth and development of each new teacher.** | Create a program that provides individualized, personalized, and contextualized support for each new teacher.<br>➤ *What is our goal for mentors working in a flexible mentoring program? (i.e. to work with each new teacher to learn about their strengths and needs and to tailor their work to quickly grow new teachers as far as they can in the time they are together).*<br><br>➤ *How do we educate mentors about the goals of mentoring so they are clear about their urgency and importance of their role?* | |
| **Mentors know how to use a set of flexible processes to guide their interactions with new teachers, gather data on classroom practice and student learning, foster reflection, and provide accountability.** | Provide mentors a set of flexible mentoring processes:<br>➤ *Where can we find or how can we create a set of flexible tools/protocols to guide mentoring work?*<br>➤ *How do we support mentors in learning about these tools, processes, and protocols in ways that will ensure mentors understand these are flexible organizers to guide high quality mentoring conversation—not forms to be filled in?*<br><br>➤ *How can we honor the professional knowledge and skill of mentors by allowing them to choose from amongst these tools/protocols in order to tailor their support to best fit the strengths, needs, and context of each new teacher while still helping all new teachers to reach rigorous professional based goals?*<br><br>➤ *How can a team of mentors support each other in developing their knowledge and skills?*<br><br>➤ *How might we create accountability for new teacher and student growth? (i.e. Set regular times to assess new teachers' work)?* | |

# Section III: Administrative Support and School Context

This section will examine the important role of school context and administrative support in mentoring new teachers. We will consider the choices knowledgeable school leaders can make that lead to increased teacher retention and positive environments for continued teacher learning, including the importance of providing new teachers with appropriate and sustainable teaching assignments; ensuring new teachers have the resources necessary to effectively teach students; fostering positive relationships between site administrators and new teachers; and deepening connections between mentors and site administrators.

It is widely understood that the principal is the key to a successful school. They are also a key factor in the success of induction programs. Site administrators set the tone and culture of the school, they oversee the hiring and placement of new teachers, they set priorities and plan professional development, and they set the schedule—all items that can have a significant impact on the way an induction program is run and how mentoring is provided to new teachers.

When site administrators understand and place value on induction work, they make intentional choices about the structure of induction programs that support mentoring and lead to increased teacher retention. For example, they build protected time into teaching schedules for frequent meetings between new teachers and mentors; provide opportunities for new teachers to plan and collaborate with other experienced teachers within their subject and grade level, or join an external network of teachers; and provide teachers with access to high-quality, long-term, job-embedded professional development.

Effective school discipline policies also provide a positive context for mentoring: When new teachers do not need to spend an inordinate amount of time worrying about student behavior, they are more likely to use their mentors to discuss instructional issues instead of dealing with ever-present crises that arise from a chaotic school environment.

Site administrators who are knowledgeable about the needs of new teachers create assignments that are appropriate for their level of experience and will allow them to succeed and thrive in their new positions instead of burning out quickly. Instead of creating a job that involves numerous preps, or that places them with the most needy students, or that is comprised of classes other teachers do not want, principals work to create positions for new teachers that will be sustainable, wherein they will be successful and that will allow them to focus on new skills with their mentor.

They also ensure that new teachers have all the necessary resources they need to effectively teach their assigned courses; they are not given a roaming position that requires them to transport their materials on a cart from room to room throughout the day, and they are not given rooms that have been pillaged by others before the arrival of the new teacher, leaving them with inadequate supplies, materials, or furniture when they begin.

Successful school leaders also believe that every teacher is capable of becoming a high-quality educator and work with the teachers to make growth happen. They place a high value on learning and speak and act in ways that convey the importance of induction, mentoring, professional learning, and teacher growth to all members of the school community. They establish professional working relationships with new teachers early in the year and help them to set goals that are aligned with site, district, state, and professional priorities. They don't depend on mentors to make growth happen and, therefore, avoid visiting new teachers. They spend time in the classrooms of new teachers observing, looking at student work, and providing feedback related to their progress toward their goals.

Effective principals also develop strong relationships with mentors and induction program leaders to ensure mentoring is aligned with school goal setting and vision. They collaborate regularly with mentors and induction program leaders to discuss issues related to new teacher development, school goals, and the integration of new teacher support into school systems and structures.

In schools where site administrators and induction program leaders are on the same page about what is in the best interest of the new teacher, both mentors and new teachers thrive. However, when induction program leaders and site administrators are not in alignment, even the best of induction programs can suffer. In a number of studies, researchers found that even when new teachers had access to well-matched mentors, administrative support was the single biggest factor in their decision to leave their school and leave teaching altogether.

Given the significant impact that principals have on mentoring success in a school, one of the most important stakeholder partnerships an induction program leader can develop is with site administrators. This partnership can allow the program director to support the principal in making the kinds of decisions about school culture, staffing, organization of professional learning, and organization of time that can lead to higher rates of teacher retention, improved school culture, and student success.

The chapters that follow will address in more detail the following ways in which site administrators can create the context for successful induction and mentoring of new teachers:

1. sustainably assigning new teachers
2. fostering positive new teacher–administrator relationships
3. deepening mentor-administrator connections

Each of these chapters includes information that both induction program leaders and site administrators can use to develop an effective working partnership that increases the likelihood of new teacher retention and, ultimately, student learning.

# 9

# Sustainably Assigning New Teachers

**Well Developed**

*Site administrators create teaching assignments with reasonable workloads for new teachers that are appropriate for their level of experience (i.e. not given the most challenging classes, multiple preps, or roving assignments).*

*New teachers are provided with the resources and materials necessary to effectively teach their assigned classes.*

In a recent op-ed, New Teacher Center CEO, Ellen Moir, writes: Despite the current focus on making sure all educators are effective, we are not setting up most new teachers to make a difference, and their students pay the price. I don't know any successful businesses that would hire entry-level grads for the most difficult positions, isolate them from coworkers, and then expect them to perform as well as more experienced colleagues. But that's exactly what we do with many new teachers who often receive the most challenging teaching assignments in the classrooms and schools whose students need the profession's best teachers.[1]

Each year, schools hire thousands of new teachers for positions that are not appropriate for those just beginning to teach. They are given assignments that include teaching multiple preps, working with the classes the more veteran teachers don't want, and, if they are lucky enough to get a classroom of their own, there are too few resources to do their job well with no chance of getting more. These promising new teachers, who until recently were optimistic teacher education students learning about what good instruction should look like, spend long hours alone trying to figure out how to put together something resembling good teaching that is going to reach the students in front of them with the limited resources at their disposal.

It is no wonder that 46 percent of them will burn out before the end of their fifth year.[2] Many will leave much sooner. While those that receive high-quality mentoring and induction may last longer, no amount of mentoring, no matter how high quality, can overcome the overwhelmingly difficult contextual issues described above.

In order for mentoring to truly have a chance at supporting new teachers, retaining them in their positions, and helping them to grow into high-quality educators, principals need to seriously consider the kinds of assignments into which the newest members of the teaching profession are placed. Creating sustainable assignments that can support new teacher and mentor success requires two things:

1. creating teaching positions that are manageable and appropriate for a new teacher's level of experience
2. ensuring teachers have the necessary resources to effectively plan and teach their assigned courses

## CREATING APPROPRIATE TEACHING POSITIONS FOR NEW TEACHERS

Unfortunately, many schools have developed a culture in which new teachers are assigned to work with lower-achieving students while more veteran teachers work with higher-achieving students. It has become common for teachers and schools to believe that having taught for a number of years earns a teacher the right to teach his or her preferred classes—which often equate with advanced placement, honors, and other "high-status" courses.

As further evidence of this disturbing trend, a study by Stanford researchers found that teachers with ten or more years of experience, as well as those who have held leadership positions, are assigned higher-achieving students on average. The study also found that lower-achieving students, who also are often minority and poor students, are most often taught by less-experienced teachers who also tend to be less effective. This inequity further exacerbates the achievement gap.[3]

This research is corroborated by program leaders who informally gather data on new teacher assignments as part of their data collection process. For example, in one district, the program leader found that new teachers were three times more likely to teach English-learner classes. When he looked further, he found that 21 percent of new teachers in the district were teaching these classes as opposed to just 7 percent of veteran teachers.[4]

This pattern of assigning more senior and effective teachers to work with high-achieving students while assigning new teachers to work primarily with low-achieving and high-need students is not only bad for students, it is also bad for teachers, schools, and society at large. Why is it that the most effective teachers in a school are not automatically assigned to the neediest students? Why is it not considered a privilege to be labeled as a teacher so effective that the school and community are willing to place their trust in you and assign you to work with those who need you the most? Why shouldn't we assign new teachers to work with students with whom they can be effective—those who are neither low-achieving, English learners, or students who are extremely high achieving (who have their own set of special needs)—while they learn the skills and knowledge they need to become highly effective so they, too, can be prepared to work with high-need students?

While there are a number of complex political factors involving school leaders, school culture, and parental involvement as well as teacher's qualifications (i.e., not all teachers are certified to teach Physics) that result in the assignment of teachers, savvy school principals understand the inherent inequity that the current system of "relegating newbies to the bottom" creates is not a sustainable way to assign teachers, nor is it an equitable one, and they will seek ways to change this culture.

When an opening becomes available, principals can use the opportunity to hire people who are right for their schools and then take stock of their staff, consider who is qualified and who is most effective, and then assign teachers in ways that will be in the best interests of both the students and the new teachers joining the staff. When at all possible:

- Create assignments that are single prep and assign new teachers to work with students who can learn from the new teacher as she grows into her new profession (i.e., are neither remedial nor advanced placement courses and do not contain all the students the other teachers do not want to teach).
- Do not assign new teachers to other duties such as sponsoring clubs, coaching sports, or serving on schoolwide teams or committees that can take time away from important planning and collaboration time in their first years.
- Provide time for new teachers to collaborate with their mentor and their colleagues as well as training for new teachers and their veteran colleagues in how to effectively collaborate with others in their grade or department so that these interactions are professionally positive and promote instructional growth. New teachers also need time to attend outside learning experiences that will support the development of their knowledge and skills in relation to their goals.

Understandably, making these kinds of adjustments can cause some challenges within a school or community at first, but it will ultimately lead to a more sustainable system of assignment that ensures new teachers have the time and space they need to learn to be effective and that all students are receiving the kind of instruction they need to succeed.

## PROVIDE NECESSARY RESOURCES
## FOR NEW TEACHER SUCCESS

Another trend that challenges the success of new teachers is a lack of resources to effectively teach their assigned classes. This can include everything from being given a roving assignment to not having enough books and desks in their classrooms.

1. *Roving Assignments.* All too often new teachers, especially those at the secondary level or who teach a specialty area, find themselves without a permanent room of their own. Instead, these teachers must load their supplies and materials onto a cart and migrate between a series of classrooms throughout the day. Without a permanent room, roving teachers lack space to keep materials, display instructional aides and student work, and often struggle to keep materials organized. This challenge, on top of the other placement concerns discussed above, can be enough to easily drive a new teacher from the classroom before the end of his or her first year.

   If a teacher must be transient, consider how to make the situation as easy as possible:

   • Consider carefully which rooms the teacher must work in. Ask questions such as: Is the teacher with whom the new teacher must share amenable? Will she be helpful and open to the needs of the new teacher? What is the minimum number of moves the teacher would need to make? Are the rooms in which the teacher is working close together?
   • Provide him with a home base close to the rooms in which he is teaching where he can store materials and complete work.
   • Mentors and site administrators can also help to facilitate conversations with the classroom teachers whose rooms the roving teacher must use to help set ground rules for use, create space for hanging materials on a more permanent basis, and negotiate other areas of challenge.
   • Check in more regularly with the teacher and mentor to ensure the situation is not becoming too overwhelming and to address additional challenges as they arise.

2. *Insufficient Materials.* Even if a new teacher is assigned to a room, it is not uncommon for that teacher to arrive on the first day of the pre-school work week only to find that the room has been picked over by the rest of the department or school, leaving no supplies, incomplete sets of materials, or insufficient furniture. Now, in addition to the other challenges that coincide with beginning the school year as a new teacher, the mentor and teacher must spend their time together finding, ordering (if this is possible), buying (often with personal funds), and borrowing what they need just to get started instead of using their time together for planning curriculum.

Principals can ease this transition by:

- developing a clear expectation that supplies belonging to a classroom should remain with that classroom, even if the teacher is in transition
- work with the department head or grade-level chair to go through the room and ensure that the new teacher will arrive to find a classroom stocked with the necessary materials, books, desks, and other supplies
- check in with mentors before school begins to ensure new teachers have everything they need to get started and that there are no missing items that would make instruction difficult

Creating sustainable teaching assignments for new teachers greatly enhances the likelihood of mentoring success because it allows new teachers to focus on what they need to grow their own practice with the support of their mentor instead of spending their energy in survival mode.

## READY TO TAKE THE NEXT STEP?

At the end of this section, there is a Discussion Guide designed to help program leaders consider the key ideas discussed in this chapter. These questions are designed to support you in beginning the important discussions about these key topics with other stakeholders and decision makers in your organization.

## NOTES

1. Ellen Moir, "Op-Ed: For First Year Teachers, It's Sink or Swim." *Take Part,* September 10, 2012. Accessed from: http://www.takepart.com/article/2012/09/10/first-year-teachers-its-sink-or-swim.

2. National Commission on Teaching and America's Future, *No Dream Denied: A Pledge to America's Children.* Washington, DC: Author, 2003. Accessed from: http://nctaf.org/wp-content/uploads/2012/01/no-dream-denied_summary_report .pdf.

3. Demetra Kalogrides, Susanna Loeb, and Tara Béteille, "Systematic Sorting: Teacher Characteristics and Class Assignments." *American Sociological Association: Sociology of Education* 86, no. 2 (2013): 103–23.

4. Josh Maisel (Fremont Union High School District Induction Program director) in conversation with the author, January 2014.

# 10

# Providing Opportunities for Planning and Collaboration with Colleagues

| Well Developed |
| --- |
| *New teachers are provided with regularly scheduled planning/collaboration time with other teachers in the same grade/subject weekly or bi-weekly.* |
| *Time with colleagues is spent in ongoing and collaborative inquiry that leads to instructional improvement and student learning.* |
| *New teachers are purposefully connected with a professional learning community that extends beyond their grade level, school, or district that supports teachers' individualized needs for ongoing professional learning.* |

To keep good teachers, school leaders need to realize that teachers crave connection, want to contribute to a group, and want to make a difference. Robert Fantilli and Douglas McDougall found in their research that new teachers perceive principals who foster and promote a collaborative culture in their school, who are available to teachers and open to questions, as being extremely effective support.[1] Similarly, Susan Kardos and Susan Moore Johnson found that principal engagement with induction—specifically creating the working conditions that facilitate sanctioned time for planning, peer observation, data analysis, and other types of professional collaboration—is essential for positive and productive professional experiences for new teachers.[2]

School leaders and mentoring programs that provide teachers this connection by finding ways to create learning communities wherein new and veteran teachers interact professionally and respectfully and are valued for their contributions are considered particularly valuable, according to many anecdotal reports. Teachers remain in teaching when they feel they belong and when they have high-quality interpersonal relationships founded on trust and respect with their colleagues. This collegial inter-change, not isolation, must become the norm for teachers if we want to keep our best and brightest in the profession.

Giving teachers time to work together may seem like a no-brainer of an idea for most people who work in education. Unfortunately, one of the harsh paradoxes of teaching is that the schools least prepared to support new teachers—that is, low-income, low-performing facilities—are the ones where most new teachers are sent. When they arrive, they often encounter an isolated, everyone-for-themselves system vastly different from the collaborative school of education or student-teaching environment they just left.

This challenge is further compounded because many Millennials, the generation now entering the teaching profession, are more team and process oriented than previous generations of teachers, and they crave a connection with their peers. This means that, from the beginning, there is a gap between the way these new teachers work best and the structure of the schools into which they are being hired.

While many of them receive mentoring in their first years that can ease the sense of isolation inherent in the profession, the period of mentor support is short and, for this generation of young employees who don't view jobs with the permanence that their parents did, a lack of meaningful connections with others dramatically increases the likelihood they'll move within their district or state looking for a position that suits them and, if they don't find one they like, they'll leave the profession altogether.

Departures among new teachers are particularly acute at those high-need schools where there's no professional continuity and the teachers don't know each other. Mentoring programs and schools need to find ways to create regular and meaningful ways for teachers to work together, to develop connections with one another, and to harness the collective power of teachers to improve student learning.

While this culture of isolation tends to be most acute in high-need schools, it is often the case in other schools as well. However, in schools where administrators understand the need for teachers to work together, time has been set aside for teachers to work together with their grade level, departments, or other school colleagues. In fact, in a recent poll of teachers, more than 75 percent of respondents said they already have common planning time, and almost as many (71 percent) said some kind of teacher-led learning teams were operating in their schools.[3]

While most school leaders see value in common planning time, helping teachers learn to use that time effectively can be challenging. One major challenge, as with many things in education, is the time to do it well. Nearly twenty-five years ago, Phillip Schlecty observed, "The one commodity teachers and administrators say they do not have enough of, even more than money, is time: time to teach, time to converse, time to think, time to plan, even time to go to the restroom or have a cup of coffee. Time is indeed precious in a school."[4]

But time alone is not enough to make common planning time useful. It only works for both veteran and new teachers when the work being done is meaningful, coordinated, collective, and collaborative. Only then can collaboration have significant and powerful impacts on teacher learning and student growth.

So how can mentor-program leaders support schools, mentors, and new teachers in making the most of planning and collaboration with colleagues, as Smith and Ingersoll suggested, no matter what type of school they work in? There are three key areas:

1. New teachers are provided with regularly scheduled planning/collaboration time with other teachers in the same grade/subject.
2. Time with colleagues is spent in ongoing and collaborative inquiry that leads to instructional improvement.
3. New teachers are purposefully connected with a professional learning community that extends beyond their grade level, school, or district that supports teachers' individualized needs for ongoing professional learning.

With the support and guidance of mentors, school leaders, and program administrators, new teachers can begin to widen their community of supportive colleagues, continue developing and improving their understanding of student needs and instructional best practices, and have the kinds of collaborative experiences that support new teachers, particularly Millennials, to remain in their classrooms, schools, and in the profession.

## NEW TEACHERS ARE PROVIDED WITH REGULARLY SCHEDULED PLANNING/COLLABORATION TIME WITH OTHER TEACHERS IN THE SAME GRADE/SUBJECT

In study after study, findings show that teachers express more satisfaction in schools when those schools give them more time to work and learn together. Teachers are happier when their schools make collaborative teacher learning a part of the workday. They also value opportunities to make teaching public through sharing with the larger community what has been learned through those collaborations. Collaboration supports sustainability because all teachers, both new and veteran, feel they are working together to benefit students and the district at large with a collegial mind-set and in a collaborative culture.

When teachers work together, the teacher's role shifts from working in isolation to working in collaboration with others. Teachers move from a teaching role to a learning and reflective role, and they build their capacity to become leaders in their school communities. Working together provides teachers with the opportunity to break down the professional isolation inherent in teaching, which can hamper the ability of teachers to build the knowledge and confidence needed to become leaders. Instead, collaboration provides teachers with an opportunity to connect with others, broaden their perspectives, and bond around a common experience.

Common planning time is designated and protected time for teachers to work with their colleagues in this way. The idea of planning time is not new, but the creation of common planning time typically requires changes to the daily schedule. Common planning time works best when teachers from the same grade level or department meet with the clear intention to use the planning time for collaboration in direct support of student learning. That time together must also be long enough and frequent enough to undertake important tasks related to improving student learning. This time must be protected time during which teachers may not be pulled to complete other administrative tasks or instructional duties that would interfere with their ability to participate in common planning time.

In a nutshell, effective teacher collaboration teams:

1. have a shared understanding of how common planning time ought to be used
2. have adequate time in the schedule to meet regularly
3. focus on instructional planning by analyzing/monitoring data to align curriculum to address the greatest areas of need and strengths
4. improve teachers' responsiveness to student needs and strengths
5. result in better/more consistent standards-based classroom instruction
6. increase the capacity of staff to collaborate effectively
7. are adequately supported by school and district administration
8. are positively impacting student learning

This means that administrators must be supportive of common planning time and make the changes in the schedule necessary to allow teachers with similar content or students to meet together regularly free from other responsibilities. They also need to find ways to teach and then support teachers in using this time together well. This includes helping teachers learn how to function as a team, how to look at and use data, how to share practice and provide each other with meaningful feedback, and how to plan together collaboratively.

When administrators have made this time available for teachers to meet, it is easier for mentors to help new teachers to make the most of this time.

They can attend departmental meetings or professional learning community meetings with new teachers, help them to debrief those experiences, and to follow up on what they learned in those meetings during their mentoring interactions. Mentors can help new teachers to quickly integrate into a community of supporters who will continue to help them build their practice, ask reflective questions, and increase student learning.

Even if the conditions in the school do not currently provide sanctioned time for collaborative work with colleagues, mentors can and should still support new teachers in beginning to build their own professional networks with their co-workers. Mentors can reach out to other teachers in the school where the new teacher works, or they can support the new teacher in making these connections to begin to build networks. They can help to gather teachers with common students or content together to talk about common needs and begin to support the teachers, including the new teacher, in building learning communities, even if they aren't part of the school administrator's plans yet.

For example, in the Fremont Union High School District in California, mentors organize lunchtime roundtable discussions for their new teachers twice each year. New teachers invite a panel of their veteran colleagues to join them for lunch (paid for by the mentoring program) and discuss the new teacher's inquiry. Not only is the discussion that occurs during these roundtables rich and helpful in shaping the new teacher's thinking, it also fosters the beginning of positive professional relationships with those veteran colleagues, which are invaluable connections for new teachers.[5]

When mentors are familiar with the school, district, or surrounding areas, they can also use their networks to reach out to others who teach the same grade or content as a new teacher or who are trying strategies the new teacher is interested in trying. They can help these teachers connect either in person through classroom visits or via technology through video conferencing or phone.

Mentor program leaders can support mentors in learning how to exercise their roles as teacher leaders to make these connections and to help them learn facilitation skills that will help mentors to make these connections and interactions run smoothly.

## TIME WITH COLLEAGUES IS SPENT IN ONGOING AND COLLABORATIVE INQUIRY THAT LEADS TO INSTRUCTIONAL IMPROVEMENT

Forming networks with colleagues is not enough, however. New teachers (and, frankly, all teachers) benefit greatly from being part of well-run, ongoing, collaborative learning experiences with their colleagues that focus on student growth. While having a mentor is an essential component of high-quality induction, new teachers also need to learn how to be part of a professional community and develop a network of colleagues who can help them continue learning, growing, and updating their practice throughout their careers and long after mentor supports have phased out of their working lives.

In 2001, Michael Garet and his colleagues reported that in a study of 1,027 public school math and science teachers in kindergarten through grade twelve, teachers learned more in teacher networks and study groups than through any other form of professional development. The teachers reported they learned more because these forms of professional learning are longer, sustained, and more intensive than shorter ones, and involve collective participation. They were also perceived by teachers as being part of a coherent professional development program unlike other professional development formats. These types of professional learning experiences and networks should not be underestimated, as many qualitative studies of new teachers report that it is strong connections with colleagues that convince them to stay in teaching and in their schools even when they are considering giving up.[6]

However, not all kinds of collaboration are equally useful. Judith Warren Little set out a continuum of collaboration from weaker to stronger forms:[7]

| Lowest | | | Highest |
| --- | --- | --- | --- |
| Scanning and storytelling- exchanging ideas, anecdotes & stories | Help and assistance- usually when asked | Sharing of materials and teaching strategies | Joint work- teachers teach, plan, or inquire into teaching together |

Continuum of Teacher Collaboration Activities

Many so-called professional learning communities (PLCs) do not focus on growing teacher knowledge and practice, but instead they merely provide a venue for teachers to vent frustrations or talk about problems at a superficial level.

Mentoring programs—and professional development programs in general—that work focus on what Laura Desimone refers to as the "Big 5":

1. content focus
2. coherence
3. collective participation
4. duration
5. active learning

Below is a brief description of each of these key areas:

1. *Content Focus.* Perhaps the most important factor in teacher growth, professional development that focuses on the development of a teacher's content knowledge and how students learn content increases teacher knowledge and skills, improves practice, and increases student achievement.

   A focus on content means two things: 1) supporting the development of a teacher's disciplinary knowledge, and 2) helping teachers to develop pedagogical content knowledge that is the consideration of how students best learn that content. Pedagogical content knowledge is different from general pedagogical knowledge in that general content knowledge applies across content, and includes such things as classroom management strategies, student engagement strategies, or the benefit of using graphic organizers or other visual representations. Pedagogical content knowledge, on the other hand, involves specific applications of general strategies and integrates a deep knowledge of the content, including anticipation of student misconceptions.

   Desimone gives the math example of using manipulatives, which is generally accepted as good pedagogy across content areas. However, if the manipulatives are not paired with deep content knowledge on the part of the teacher, and if the teacher doesn't understand how to use the manipulatives in specific ways to support the development of students' rich mathematical understanding, to explore student thinking about math concepts, and to find multiple ways to approach a problem, including correcting misconceptions, they do not necessarily lead to increased student achievement. (See chapter 3 for an example from history.)

2. *Coherence.* Professional development for teachers is often criticized because the events seem disconnected from one another both in time and in focus. Coherent professional learning has three key components:

   - It builds on what teachers already know. It is targeted neither too high nor too low, but is aligned to a teacher's zone of proximal development.
   - It is aligned with national, state, and district goals. This is a careful balancing act in that what a school has chosen as an area of focus may not be what the district or state have prioritized. This can lead to incoherence and frustration from teachers. Mentors and school leaders need to consider how to keep a focus narrow yet aligned.

- It is sustained over time. Professional developers and school/program leaders need to ask the question, "How is conversation about the professional development event sustained after the event is over?" Without this sustained dialogue, implementation could be shallow.

3. *Collective Participation.* Adult learning theory tells us that the most effective learning is collaborative and self-directed. Teachers need time to work and learn together with others in the same school, grade, or department. This work needs to be job embedded, and it needs to be structured to produce meaningful discussion that leads to improved teaching and student learning.

4. *Duration.* One-time learning experiences are not enough to change teaching practice and improve student learning. Yet many schools' professional development programs consist of one-shot seminars on a smattering of topics over the course of a year. Teachers may leave with a few interesting ideas or practices, but they rarely translate into practice. If program leaders and school administrators want to make a change, time to learn and work together around a topic need to happen frequently and for a sufficient period of time to actually make progress.

5. *Active Learning.* Teachers need to be active in their learning. Too often teachers are subjected to "sit-and-get" professional development, which has been shown to be the least productive kind of teaching we can do, especially with adults. Teachers need to be engaged and feel ownership in the learning, otherwise the learning will not translate into meaningful changes in practice or student learning in the classrooms.[8]

When considered in the planning of professional development experiences, including mentoring interactions and PLCs, these five areas can support a program, school, or district in creating the kind of professional development that feels meaningful and relevant to teachers and can truly move practice and student learning forward.

## NEW TEACHERS ARE PURPOSEFULLY CONNECTED WITH A PROFESSIONAL LEARNING COMMUNITY THAT EXTENDS BEYOND THEIR GRADE LEVEL, SCHOOL, OR DISTRICT THAT SUPPORTS TEACHERS' INDIVIDUALIZED NEEDS FOR ONGOING PROFESSIONAL LEARNING

Whether schools have created these collaborative structures or not, new teachers also benefit from extending their professional learning community beyond the confines of their school. Mentors can help new teachers to connect virtually with others through online communities. Many professional groups have chat rooms and other ways to connect teachers across the country who are teaching the same content or grade level.

Some organizations are using Twitter, LinkedIn, and other social media to create virtual platforms wherein new teachers can "chat" with others who are in a similar phase in their career and get advice and support. Some organize new teachers into content- or grade-alike groups with discussions moderated by a mentor with knowledge in this area. Some organize these discussions into threads that focus on a topic or issue of the month around which new teachers and mentors can share their thoughts. These connections with others both new and veteran who can provide them ideas, resources, and support long after the mentor is gone help to build the kind of networks teachers crave.

While the idea of an online community being an important support for a new teacher may seem odd to teachers and leaders of a certain generation, Millennials are unique in that these online connections can sometimes be more powerful than the in-person ones and, therefore, it is important not to forget this often-neglected component of teacher collaboration.

## MAKING MENTORING WORK FOR YOU

Mentoring programs would do well to remember that the work they do with new teachers, while incredibly important, is only for a short while. To survive and thrive beyond the early years of their career, new teachers need supports from colleagues both in their schools and beyond. Mentors and program leaders need to remember the important task they have of helping new teachers to make those strong connections so that they have help and support long after the new teacher has stepped out of the picture. Mentoring programs that work need to remember the following key areas when planning for new teacher collaboration:

1. Program leaders must educate and advocate for common planning and collaboration time for teachers who work in the same grade or subject area. If common planning time exists, support mentors in learning how to help new teachers make the best possible use of common planning time.
2. Program leaders need to support mentors in understanding that an important part of a mentor's job is to help new teachers make connections with their colleagues and support them in developing collegial skills in order to build professional support networks that extend beyond the mentor.

3. Support site administrators in developing or improving teacher-led learning teams organized around ongoing collaborative inquiry that leads to instructional improvement.
4. Work with site administrators to integrate new teachers into existing teacher-led learning teams in ways that will support new teacher learning and meaningful collaboration with colleagues.
5. If teacher-led learning teams do not exist in a school, mentors can develop professional learning teams for groups of new teachers focused on context, content, or other common experiences that will help new teachers network with each other and learn the skills needed to be members of a professional community. Invite site administrators to visit and observe these meetings as a model for what whole-school professional learning communities could look like.
6. Program leaders and mentors can work with site and district leaders to learn about professional learning opportunities that connect with school and new teachers' individual learning goals, such as districtwide professional development, subject-matter conferences, and online professional networks. Work together to find ways to make these doable options that can expand the professional knowledge and network of the new teacher.

## READY TO TAKE THE NEXT STEP?

At the end of this section, there is a Discussion Guide designed to help program leaders consider the key ideas discussed in this chapter. These questions are designed to support you in beginning the important discussions about these key topics with other stakeholders and decision makers in your organization.

## NOTES

1. Robert D. Fantilli and Douglas E. McDougall, "A Study of Novice Teachers: Challenges and Supports in the First Years." *Teaching and Teacher Education* 25, no. 6 (2009): 814–25.
2. Susan M. Kardos and Susan Moore Johnson, "On Their Own and Presumed Expert: New Teachers' Experience with Their Colleagues." *Teachers College Record* 109, no. 9 (2007): 2083–2106.
3. Linda Darling-Hammond, Ruth Chung Wei, and Christy Marie Johnson, "Teacher Preparation and Teacher Learning: A Changing Policy Landscape." In *Handbook of Education Policy Research*, edited by Gary Sykes, Barbara L. Schneider, and David N. Plank, 613–36. New York: American Educational Research Association and Routledge, 2009.

4. Phillip C. Schlechty, *Schools for the Twenty-First Century: Leadership Imperatives for Educational Reform*. San Francisco, CA: Jossey-Bass Inc., 1990, 73.

5. Josh Maisel (Fremont Union High School District Induction Program director) in conversation with the author, January 2014.

6. Michael S. Garet, Andrew C. Porter, Laura Desimone, Beatrice F. Birman, and Kwang Suk Yoon, "What Makes Professional Development Effective? Results from a National Sample of Teachers." *American Educational Research Journal* 38, no. 4 (Winter 2001): 915–45.

7. Judith W. Little, "Understanding Data Use Practice Among Teachers: The Contribution of Micro-Process Studies." *American Journal of Education* 118, no. 2 (2012): 143–66.

8. Laura Desimone, "Improving Impact Studies of Teachers' Professional Development: Toward Better Conceptualizations and Measures." *Educational Researcher* 38, no. 3 (April 2009): 181–99.

# 11

# Deepening Mentor-Administrator Connections

---

**Well Developed**

*Mentors, program leaders, and site-based administrators meet regularly to learn about and discuss issues related to new teacher development, school goals, and integration of new teacher support into school systems and structures.*

---

Mentoring programs that work create regular opportunities to communicate with school and district administrators to help them learn about and understand the mentoring program and the resulting benefits for the new teacher and the school, as well as the role of the mentor and the needs of new teachers both generally and individually. Betty Achinstein confirms in her research that transparent communication among the principal, mentor, and new teacher is of high value to new teachers.[1]

These open lines of communication are also important for mentor program leaders and the mentors to learn about the schools and districts in which they work, their unique context, and their goals for student achievement and teacher development.

Through regular communication, the mentor and the school administrator develop a partnership with the well-being and success of the new teacher and her students as a common focus. This section will focus on three key areas that can help to deepen this important relationship between mentors and administrators:

1. building a relationship through regularity of interaction
2. learning about, aligning, and integrating new teacher support systems
3. advocating for new teachers, three-way conversations between the mentor, teacher, and school administrators (triad conversations), and other interactions with administrators

Let's look at each of these areas in turn and consider how they can develop effective partnerships between mentors and school administrators.

## BUILDING A RELATIONSHIP THROUGH
## REGULARITY OF INTERACTION

As with all relationships, the more often mentors and site administrators communicate, the better the relationship becomes. Research shows that when mentors and site administrators meet, mentors become more knowledgeable about the goals and needs of the school as well as developing a respect for the complexity of the administrators' role. Administrators learn more about the work of the mentor. Through these learning interactions, the pair are more likely to find ways to better align their work in support of the new teachers in the building. Program requirements for how often mentors and site administrators meet varies widely from one to two times a year to monthly. In the mentoring program run out of Stanford University, mentors and school administrators met quarterly to discuss upcoming activities, to learn about school initiatives, and to align and integrate their work with new teachers.

These meetings may be short check-ins, or longer learning and problem-solving sessions. Some induction programs have developed an administrator handbook to help site administrators learn about the mentoring program and to serve as a guide for planning a sequence of ongoing conversations between the mentor and the administrator. Here is an example of one possible sequence:

**Table 11.1. Sample Mentor-Administrator Yearly Meeting Agenda**

| Date | Possible Topics for Discussion |
|---|---|
| August–September | • Introductions<br>• Set calendar of meetings for year<br>• Share strategies for helping new teachers learn about school context<br>• Share basics about mentor roles and responsibilities and confidentiality<br>• Learn about school goals, priorities<br>• Learn about time lines for new teacher goal setting and observation (work to build alignment, if possible)<br>• Review learnings and agreements from today and time for next meeting |
| October–November | • Check-ins about initial observations, goal setting. Elicit ideas from site administrator about strengths and needs of new teacher (Maintaining the confidentiality of the new teacher is paramount here!)<br>• Share about tools and strategies mentor is using to support new teacher. Work to build understanding about the importance of mentoring and formative support for new teachers<br>• Work to build alignment between what the administrator needs/values and what the mentor/new teacher is working on<br>• Check in about any upcoming school-specific dates of which the mentor should be aware (i.e., professional development, holidays, school events, etc.)<br>• Review learnings and agreements from today and time for next meeting |

*(continued)*

| Date | Possible Topics for Discussion |
|------|-------------------------------|
| January–February | • Check-ins about observations, review of goals at midyear. Elicit ideas from site administrator about strengths and needs of new teacher (Remember to remain confidential!)<br>• May wish to have new teacher join this meeting to share about successes from fall, share portfolio or samples of work<br>• Share about tools and strategies mentor is using to support new teacher. Work to build understanding about the importance of mentoring and formative support for new teachers<br>• Work to build alignment between what the administrator needs/values and what the mentor/new teacher are working on<br>• Check in about any upcoming school-specific dates of which the mentor should be aware (i.e., professional development, holidays, events, etc.)<br>• Review learnings and agreements from today and time for next meeting<br>• Ask for feedback about meetings this fall. What worked? What didn't? How can you make these meetings more useful next year? |
| March–April | • Check-ins about observations, plans for remainder of year, final evaluations, plans for rehire, and more. Elicit ideas from site administrator about strengths and needs of new teacher (Remember to remain confidential!)<br>• Share about tools and strategies mentor is using to support new teacher Work to build understanding about the importance of mentoring and formative support for new teachers<br>• Work to build alignment between what the administrator needs/values and what the mentor/new teacher are working on<br>• Check in about any upcoming school-specific dates of which the mentor should be aware (i.e., professional development, holidays, events, etc.)<br>• Review learnings and agreements from today and time for next meeting |
| May–June | • Check-ins about observations, plans for remainder of year, final evaluations, plans for rehire, and more. Elicit ideas from site administrator about strengths and needs of new teacher (Remember to remain confidential!)<br>• May wish to have new teacher join this meeting to share about successes, share portfolio or samples of work<br>• Share about tools and strategies mentor is using to support new teacher. Work to build understanding about the importance of mentoring and formative support for new teachers<br>• Check in about any upcoming school-specific dates of which the mentor should be aware (i.e., professional development, end of year events, etc.)<br>• Review learnings and agreements from today<br>• Ask for feedback about meetings this year. What worked? What didn't? How can you make these meetings more useful next year? |

For mentoring programs that work across multiple schools and districts, program leaders may also wish to find ways to bring school and district administrators together periodically to learn about their needs and priorities and educate their partners about the work of the mentoring program. For example, the Santa Cruz/Silicon Valley New Teacher Project (SC/SVNTP) in California is a consortium program providing mentoring support to a group of more than twenty-five districts and charter organizations. Six times each year, the project hosts Steering Committee Meetings during which representatives from each of the partner charter schools or districts and university partners meet to learn about the project's work with new teachers, to share about areas of importance in the partnering districts, and to consider next steps that might be taken to further align the work of SC/SVNTP and its partners. These meetings are well attended, deepen working relationships across diverse partners, and always lead to improved understanding and collaboration.

However and whenever these meetings happen, they create the conditions for the development of trust and understanding on which later meetings about more challenging topics can be built.

Between these face-to-face meetings, it is also valuable for mentors and site administrators to keep open lines of communication via email or phone. Site administrators, for example, may wish to invite mentors to join a school-based professional development or staff meeting about a topic that is of interest to the new teacher, or to share about something that happened at the school that impacts the new teacher. Conversely, mentors, especially those who are not based in the school, may want to ask a quick question about a policy or procedure, or to inform the site administrator about an upcoming professional development opportunity that may be of interest to the new teacher and other staff members.

These regular interactions both face to face and via other forms of communication help the mentor and the site administrator to remain on the same page and create alignment around the new teachers' support.

## LEARNING ABOUT, ALIGNING, AND INTEGRATING NEW TEACHER SUPPORT SYSTEMS

In order to align supports for the new teacher, mentors and principals need to take the time to learn from each other and find common places where their work overlaps. Mentors might ask site administrators about the goals and priorities of the school; programs, structures, and systems in place; and time lines for goal setting and observation for new teachers. Mentors might want to share about the theory behind their program, what mentors can and cannot do, and the kinds of processes and tools they use in their work with new teachers. Through these learning discussions, mentors and site administrators can find places to further align and integrate the mentoring program into their school.

For example, before the mentor and new teacher coassess a set of professional teaching standards and set goals together, the mentor may want to talk with the site administrator to find out about what the school's goals are as well as the site administrator's time line for setting goals with the staff. If the mentoring program and the school are using the same standards, the mentor and principals can work together to choose one or a subset of those standards on which they'd like the new teacher to focus, and then the mentor can work with the new teacher to set goals before coming to the meeting with the administrator.

Or, the mentor can sit in on the goal-setting meeting with the principal and the new teacher so that she can hear the needs and areas of focus that are of priority to the principal and can plan to support the new teacher around those goals afterward. There are many other possible ways this small example might play out, but the point is that communication between the mentor and the site administrator about processes and priorities can improve alignment and integration of the mentoring program's work into the school's work from the beginning.

Mentors also need to communicate with site administrators about the rationale for the confidential nature of the mentoring relationship. In order for new teachers to take the risks necessary for them to grow in their practice, they need to know that the mentor is not going to share what they see and hear with their evaluator. To ensure confidentiality, mentors need to check that they are not compromising their confidential relationship with new teachers during meetings with site administrators. They need to learn about how to keep their body language and responses nonjudgmental.

Even nodding one's head in agreement to an administrator's positive or negative comment about a new teacher can be a breach of confidentiality, as are statements such as, "She is a great teacher." On the other hand, sharing facts about the class, content standards, or teacher attendance at an IEP meeting honors discretion. The only times mentors can share information without the new teacher in the room is either with the consent of the new teacher or if there is something dangerous or detrimental for kids happening that causes serious concern.

Being clear about confidentiality at the beginning of a working relationship between the mentor and the site administrator also makes it less likely that the site administrator will push a mentor for information about a new teacher later and, if that does happen, it makes it much easier for the mentor to remind the site administrator gently about confidentiality. A principal who understands and respects this confidentiality can continue to deepen the trusting relationship between the mentor, new teacher, and the site administrator.

A note about confidentiality: The latter of these two situations can be excruciating for mentors, especially when the new teacher is not open to critical feedback from the mentor and no improvement seems to be happening. It is even more challenging when administrators are not aware of the situation and give the teacher glowing reports. How mentors deal with situations like this is tricky business. How does the mentor maintain confidentiality in these situations but still find ways to help the new teacher improve? Should the mentor maintain confidentiality in these situations?

The best-case scenario involves mentors finding ways to encourage site administrators to visit the new teacher's classroom regularly enough so that the administrator can see for himself the situation and to strongly suggest improvements that give the mentor traction with the new teacher. Many program leaders report that conversations around confidentiality and when/if it should be violated is one of the biggest dilemmas mentors in their program face. Therefore, it is important for program leaders to help mentors in learning how to navigate these tricky situations armed with knowledge, strategies, and with grace.

These meetings between mentors and site administrators also give mentors an opportunity to help site administrators value and respect the work of the mentor and the mentoring program and to consider ways to communicate that to their staff and community. When school administrators value the work of mentors, they are more likely, for example, to build time into teaching schedules for frequent meetings between new teachers and mentors.[2] Mentoring works best when it is a deeply aligned and integrated part of the school culture and not a stand-alone or add-on program. When mentors and site administrators work together, understand each others' work, and find ways to make the two programs work seamlessly together, it is easier for the new teacher to take the work seriously and to see it as a component of the support system offered to them by the school.

## ADVOCATING FOR NEW TEACHERS, TRIADS, AND OTHER INTERACTIONS WITH ADMINISTRATORS

Apart from regular check-in meetings with site administrators, there are sometimes other reasons mentors and site administrators meet. Because mentors and principals have worked together to build trusting relationships and have developed an understanding and appreciation for each other in these other interactions, when something challenging arises, mentors and principals can work together to address the issue and create aligned support for the new teacher.

There are times when new teachers experience challenging working conditions and, because of their newness, they may lack some perspective on what is appropriate to expect in the way of working conditions. Or, if they are aware that the condition is challenging, they are often hesitant to say anything to the principal or make requests for fear that they won't seem competent in front of their new boss or because they lack the professional skills to approach their administrator. Through the development of strong communication channels with the administrator, the mentor can be an *advocate* for the new teacher. For example, effective school discipline policies contribute to a positive experience for new teachers. When new teachers do not need to spend an inordinate amount of time worrying about student behavior, they are more likely to use their time with their mentor to discuss instructional issues.[3] Therefore, mentors may choose to advocate on behalf of new teachers when they see disciplinary issues that reach beyond the classroom of the new teacher, usually with explicit permission from the new teacher. Other examples may include advocating about particular challenges in scheduling, classroom limitations, or resources that are needed, with the permission of the new teacher. Together the mentor and site administrator can seek positive ways to address the issues and create the best possible circumstances for the new teacher and her students.

There are other occasions when the mentor, the site administrator, and the new teacher may want to meet together. Sometimes called a *triad meeting*, these three-way meetings allow mentors, principals, and new teachers to meet together to learn about each other and the mentoring program, celebrate a success, or discuss a challenge. Mentors can meet independently with the administrator and the new teacher to learn about what will be discussed and to prep the new teacher for the meeting. While mentors, because of their confidential role, may not share their own impressions of the new teacher during these triad meetings, mentors can facilitate conversation between the administrator and the new teacher and support new teachers as they share about themselves and their practice with the principal. They can also listen as the site administrator shares her goals for the new teacher and next steps to be taken and can follow up with the new teacher afterward to debrief the conversation and to ensure there is follow through in making the changes or implementing the strategies the principal discussed.

One note of caution about triad meetings as well as other mentor-principal meetings: While it is important for mentors to serve as advocates on behalf of their new teachers from time to time, program leaders need to make sure mentors understand that triad meetings, as well as other meetings with site administrators, are not a time to "call out" principals about their decisions. For example, a triad meeting is not the place for a mentor to question a principal's decision to not renew a new teacher's contract for the following year. The mentor may not be privy to all of the reasons behind such a decision, and such a confrontation can destroy trust between a mentor and a principal as well as make a principal less willing to work with mentors and new teacher support programs in the future.

Each of these interactions supports the deepening of the relationship between the mentor and the site administrator, the alignment of the mentor's work with the schools' goals, and provides more integrated support for the new teacher.

## BUILDING RELATIONSHIPS WITH OTHERS WHO WORK WITH NEW TEACHERS

Mentoring programs also need to find ways to align themselves with others who provide professional development and support to new teachers. This might include instructional coaches, central office staff, and other professional developers. Mentoring program leaders need to seek out, build relationships, and develop ways to communicate with these other people. Doing so helps to develop understanding of what each support provider's role is in relation to new teachers and to create a coherent and aligned vision of what excellent teaching and learning looks like across an entire career. This knowledge allows all parties to align their services so new teachers are not spending precious time being inundated with people in their rooms and meetings with various support providers that they must attend.

## MAKING MENTORING WORK FOR YOU

Encouraging school administrators to provide strong support for mentoring programs is crucial to new teachers' success. When mentors, program leaders, and site-based administrators meet regularly to learn about each other's needs and priorities and to discuss issues related to new teacher development and the integration of new teacher support into the school's systems and structures, new teachers receive mentoring that is tailored to fit the individual and contextual needs of the new teacher. When new teachers feel they are highly supported by their administrators, they are more likely to stay in teaching and at a school than when they feel that support is not present.

To create a strong working relationship, mentoring programs that work keep the following items in mind:

1. Plan to meet regularly. Support mentors in scheduling meetings with site administrators at least every six to eight weeks. It is often best to schedule these meetings at the beginning of the year or at the end of the previous meeting when everyone has their calendars in front of them. Program leaders may also wish to attend these meetings periodically as well.
2. Create an agenda for each meeting that includes time to learn about school goals, priorities, and events; to share mentoring processes; and to discuss the needs of new teachers individually and collectively in order to align new teacher support.
3. Be clear about the importance of the confidential relationship between the mentor and new teacher and the need to respect that confidentiality. Support mentors in understanding what is and what is not a breach of confidentiality when talking with site administrators.
4. Support the school administrator in understanding the important role mentors play in the lives of new teachers, and explain the need for site administrators to clearly communicate the value of induction, mentoring, and ongoing professional learning to their staff.
5. Help mentors know how and when it may be appropriate to advocate on behalf of new teachers. Support mentors in developing the language and protocols for asking site administrators for support.
6. Help mentors know how and when it may be appropriate to hold triad meetings between the principal-mentor and new teacher. Support mentors in developing the skills and processes to effectively plan for, facilitate, and debrief these meetings.
7. Reach out to others who work with new teachers to learn about their programs and to share about your work. Find ways to align and consolidate services for new teachers so they are not overwhelmed with too much support.

## READY TO TAKE THE NEXT STEP?

At the end of this section, there is a Discussion Guide designed to help program leaders consider the key ideas discussed in this chapter. These questions are designed to support you in beginning the important discussions about these key topics with other stakeholders and decision makers in your organization.

## NOTES

1. Betty Achinstein, "New Teacher and Mentor Political Literacy: Reading, Navigating, and Transforming Induction Contexts." *Teachers and Teaching: Theory and Practice* 12, no. 2 (2006): 123–38.

2. Stephen H. Fletcher, Michael Strong, and Anthony Villar, "An Investigation of the Effects of Variations in Mentor-Based Induction on the Performance of Students in California." *Teachers College Record* 110, no. 10 (2008): 2271–89.

3. Marjorie E. Wechsler, Kyra Caspary, Daniel C. Humphrey, and Kavita K. Matsko, "Examining the Effects of New Teacher Induction." Menlo Park, CA: SRI International, 2010.

# 12

# Fostering Positive New Teacher–Administrator Relationships

**Well Developed**

*Site administrators work to develop relationships with new teachers early in the year, help them set appropriate goals, observe teachers regularly in a formative capacity, and provide timely, positive, and useful feedback related to their progress towards those goals.*

The school context in which teachers spend their first years can affect the kind of support they receive. In a number of studies, researchers found that even when new teachers had access to well-matched mentors, administrative support and other school factors made a big difference in the effectiveness of induction and the rate of teacher turnover. Interestingly, most school administrators feel they are supportive of new teachers, even when their new teachers report they are not.

There are three ways mentors and program leaders support the development of positive and supportive relationships between new teachers and school administrators:

1. support school administrators in connecting early in the year with new teachers
2. support school administrators in setting manageable but rigorous goals in collaboration with new teachers
3. support school administrators in providing new teachers with regular feedback related to their progress toward their identified goals

Let's look at each of these in turn and consider how fostering a positive relationship between new teachers and their administrators is beneficial for all parties.

## SUPPORT SCHOOL ADMINISTRATORS IN CONNECTING EARLY IN THE YEAR WITH NEW TEACHERS

New teachers stay in a school more often when they feel they have a strong and trusting working relationship with their site administrator. However, this can be hard thing for principals to prioritize early in the school year. As you know, the beginning of the school year is a hectic time for school administrators. There is much to do as schools open and staff and students return. It is easy for orienting and inducting new teachers, let alone building relationships with new teachers, to fall down to the bottom of a school administrator's to-do list. This can leave new teachers feeling alone and unsupported. That feeling of isolation can be further compounded if they were not assigned a mentor before the school year began.

Mentors can support school administrators in building procedures that can help new teachers start the year off right both in the profession and also with the site administrator. One way to begin well is to ensure each school provides an orientation run by the site administration that meets the needs of new teachers. While many districts offer an orientation to new teachers either when they are first hired or at the start of the year, these orientations do not help new teachers to get to know and begin to become a part of their particular school. A strong orientation to a school includes an understanding of:

- the mission and vision of the school
- site norms and expectations
- site procedures (i.e., keys, emergency procedures, attendance, translation services, breaks, lunch, signing in/out, substitutes)
- forms (i.e., report cards, accident reports, referrals, ordering supplies)
- technology and resources (i.e., online grade book, smart boards, computers, book room, standards)

It also includes a tour of the site and introductions to key staff (custodians, office staff) as well as the names and contact information of people who can be of support. These orientations give new teachers and principals a chance to get to know each other in a larger (possibly safer) group setting and give new teachers an opportunity to hear explicitly what the school and administrator are "about." This is what some mentors call the "how we do things here" talk, which is so important for new teachers to hear as they begin to integrate into their new professional community.

Many mentoring programs have created a checklist with topics for effective site orientations that they provide to school administrators to help them develop these important first meetings. Some school-based mentors also help to plan and deliver these orientations. However, even if the mentor is the primary planner of these meetings, it is important for principals to be present, to be seen as involved, and to be available for questions during these initial meetings.

In addition to this group orientation, school administrators also need to find time to connect with new teachers individually. Informal visits, an open-door policy, and intentionally finding time to get to know new teachers can all lead to a successful beginning. Some administrators host "new teacher lunches" regularly, which provide new teachers and administrators a great opportunity to have positive interactions in a social situation as well as to get to know each other and build trust. These experiences make it much more likely that a new teacher will be willing to approach the principal if he needs something because they have this positive relational foundation.

Even when administrators do not take on this role, mentors can still help to foster these relationships by beginning the year with a triad meeting (see previous section for description), wherein the new teacher, site administrator, and mentor can get to know each other. Mentors can also help by creating regular group mentoring or new teacher professional development/professional learning community sessions wherein all the new mentors in a school or district meet together. Mentors can then invite administrators to join those meetings to learn about the mentoring program and also to build relationships with new teachers. When new teachers see site administrators in these sessions, they come to view the administrator as more open and approachable as well as knowledgeable and sympathetic to their needs.

Finally, mentors can encourage site administrators to visit the classrooms of new teachers and can encourage new teachers to invite the site administrator to visit on days where there is something interesting happening in the classroom.

Each of these early interactions between new teachers and site administrators helps to foster a positive working relationship wherein the new teacher feels known and supported by their school leaders.

## SUPPORT SCHOOL ADMINISTRATORS IN SETTING MANAGEABLE BUT RIGOROUS GOALS IN COLLABORATION WITH NEW TEACHERS

Mentors are trained by their programs to work with new teachers to set meaningful and reasonable standards-based goals. Mentors know that these goals set the stage for their work together by giving it urgency and direction as well as providing signposts for success. While many savvy site administrators know how to help teachers create goals and are often eager to do so, a lack of time and other responsibilities often make goal setting with new teachers a low priority.

Through regular meetings with school administrators, mentors can support site administrators in looking over school or programmatic goals and preplanning which goals should be of most importance to new teachers. Mentors can also help site administrators to create a time line for goal setting and can work with new teachers ahead of those meetings to coassess against standards and consider possible goals. They can also help new teachers to arrive at their goal-setting meetings with site administrators prepared to lead those discussions and share their ideas. When new teachers enter meetings with site administrators knowing what to expect and what they want to say, it takes some of the fear away and allows the pair to have rich dialogue about the teacher's goals and progress that might not otherwise occur.

## SUPPORT SCHOOL ADMINISTRATORS IN PROVIDING NEW TEACHERS WITH REGULAR FEEDBACK RELATED TO THEIR PROGRESS TOWARD THEIR IDENTIFIED GOALS

Years of California state induction survey data show that new teachers report site administrators visit their classroom an average of one to three times per year, whereas site administrators report visiting an average of five to seven times per year. Why the discrepancy? One possibility is the feedback new teachers receive. Site administrators, for example, may be reporting each time they enter a new teacher's classroom, whereas new teachers only remember and count when they are formally observed and given feedback. If this is so, how can mentors help site administrators to make better use of each visit to a new teacher's classroom?

Even when principals do find time to set goals with new teachers, providing feedback and coaching around those goals is often a challenging task. Again, the press of time that most site administrators feel means classroom observations do not happen as often as either the school administrator or the teacher would like. Further, many principals say that they have received little training about conducting classroom observations and providing meaningful feedback, meaning that their visits, when they do occur, do not always lead to satisfactory outcomes.

Mentors who work in successful mentoring programs have been given a great deal of knowledge and skill in gathering classroom observation data and providing feedback to new teachers focused on goals. In some mentoring programs, mentors and program leaders are actually teaching site administrators how to conduct effective observations! As Laura Gschwend, former director of the Santa Cruz/Silicon Valley New Teacher Project in California, put it, "Mentors are incredibly important because they are capable of leading from the middle."[1] When meeting with site administrators, mentors can share about these practices and tools and can encourage site administrators to use them as well.

Mentors can also volunteer to facilitate pre- and post-observation meetings for formal observations with the site administrator and the new teacher to encourage discussions that focus on how observational data gathered about the teacher's instructional practices and students' work during those observations shows evidence of progress toward the new teacher's goals. Mentors can encourage site administrators to hold at least four of these more formal observations during the year, and they can also encourage site administrators to provide feedback related to goals when they visit informally as well.

## MAKING MENTORING WORK FOR YOU

Mentoring programs that work are only as good as the support they get from administrators. Encouraging and supporting school administrators to build strong and trusting professional partnerships with new teachers wherein they get to know new teachers, help them to set meaningful goals, and give them feedback on those goals helps new teachers feel cared for and supported. When the research shows that new teachers often name a lack of support by their administrator as their reason for leaving a school or the profession,[2] mentors and program leaders need to make sure that these relationships are in order so they have a supportive context in which to work.

Program leaders and mentors can help foster a positive working relationship between new teachers and site administrators by:

1. encouraging and supporting site administrators to hold a site-based orientation for new teachers that helps them begin to understand and connect with their new context as well as begin to connect with their site administrator. Programs can also help by creating a checklist of important topics to cover during these orientations and/or by helping to facilitate them.

2. reminding site administrators of the importance of getting to know each new teacher in his or her building. Mentors can encourage the development of these relationships through triad meetings, inviting site administrators to periodically join new teacher meetings, and through other venues.

3. working with site administrators to align goal-setting processes with teaching standards, school instructional goals, and the professional interests/needs of the new teacher. Align goal-setting time lines so that mentors can work ahead of time with new teachers to coassess and set goals in preparation for these meetings to encourage thoughtful and fruitful conversations between new teachers and site administrators.

4. encouraging, teaching, and providing tools to site administrators that will help them to make regular, meaningful formal and informal visits to new teachers' classrooms. Help them learn how to gather concrete data and give feedback that includes manageable steps for improving practice connected to the goals of the new teacher. Mentors may also offer to facilitate pre- and postobservation conversations to support the alignment of observational feedback and goals in a meaningful way.

## READY TO TAKE THE NEXT STEP?

At the end of this section, there is a Discussion Guide designed to help program leaders consider the key ideas discussed in this chapter. These questions are designed to support you in beginning the important discussions about these key topics with other stakeholders and decision makers in your organization.

## NOTES

1. Laura Gschwend (former director of the Santa Cruz/Silicon Valley New Teacher Project) in conversation with the author, November 2013.

2. Thomas Smith and Richard Ingersoll, "What Are the Effects of Induction and Mentoring on Beginning Teacher Turnover?" *American Educational Research Journal* 41, no. 3 (2004): 681–714.

# Section III Discussion Guide

## SECTION CONCLUSION

Creating effective partnerships between mentors, induction leaders, and site administrators is key to developing a successful mentoring program. In order to truly make mentoring work, the principal must be more than someone who hires new teachers and who may possibly assign mentors to new teachers. They must also take a primary role in leading the induction effort, ensuring the new teacher is successful and the students are achieving. In all schools, but especially in hard-to-staff schools, the research finds that teachers choose to remain at schools where principals are effective leaders who create sustainable working environments. They:

1. hire the right people and put them in the right roles
2. provide them the resources necessary to do their jobs well
3. support them in working together collectively to achieve a common goal
4. support them individually to achieve their own professional goals
5. work with other support providers to align their work in support of their goals for the school, teachers, and students

Mentoring program leaders and site administrators need to work together to ensure new teachers enter the profession in a school where the administration has put systems such as these in place to support them. When they do, new teachers are more than three times as likely to stay in teaching and in that school than a new teacher without those site-based supports. This is true even if the new teacher has a high-quality mentor.

No two mentoring programs are exactly alike, as each caters to the individual culture and specific needs of its unique school or district. Therefore, this book cannot provide a prescriptive way to build a mentoring program that works. Instead, below, and on the following pages you will find Part III of the *Making Mentoring Work* Discussion Guide, which includes some guiding questions you can ask yourself and your stakeholders in order to help you build a mentoring program that works for you. This resource is intended for use by induction program leaders as both a self-reflection tool as well as a guide for organizing conversations with stakeholders about the state of their working relationships with site administrators.

| III. Successful mentoring programs work in coordination with school-based leaders to create a working environment conducive to new teacher success. | | |
|---|---|---|
| **Successful Implementation** | **Questions to Consider** | **Ideas Generated for Program Development** |
| **A. Sustainably Assignment of New Teachers** | | |
| Site administrators create teaching assignments for new teachers that are appropriate for their level of experience and provide a sustainable workload. | Working Conditions<br>➢ *How can mentors and induction program leaders communicate the importance of positive working conditions on new teacher development to all site administrators?*<br><br>➢ *How can mentors and induction program leaders support site administrators in developing working conditions that are favorable to new teacher and induction program success?* | |
| New teachers are provided with the resources and materials necessary to effectively teach their assigned classes. | Sustainable Teaching Assignments<br>➢ *How can mentors and induction program leaders communicate the importance of creating sustainable assignments for new teachers to all site administrators?*<br><br>➢ *How can mentors and induction program leaders support site administrators in developing a policy of sustainable assignment for new teachers in their schools?*<br><br>➢ *How can mentors and induction program leaders support site administrators in creating policies/structures/protocols that will ensure all new teachers are provided needed materials to carry out their teaching assignments?*<br><br>➢ *How can mentors and induction program leaders support principals in organizing the school schedule to maximize the ability of the mentor to have an impact on teachers?* | |

(*continued*)

| B. Providing Opportunities for Planning and Collaboration with Colleagues | | |
|---|---|---|
| **Successful Implementation** | **Questions to Consider** | **Ideas Generated for Program Development** |
| New teachers are provided with regularly scheduled planning/collaboration time with other teachers in the same grade/subject. | Common Planning Time: <br> ➤ *Do our schools provide common planning and collaboration time for all teachers who work in the same subject or grade? If not, how might we educate and advocate for common planning and collaboration time?* <br><br> ➤ *How are mentors helping new teachers make the best possible use of common planning time? How can we support mentors in doing more on this front?* | |
| Time with colleagues is spent in ongoing and collaborative inquiry that leads to instructional improvement. | Connecting with colleagues in school to improve teaching and learning: <br> ➤ *Are mentors helping new teachers to develop professional connections with other colleagues? How might we support mentors in understanding that an important part of a mentor's job is to help new teachers make connections with their colleagues and support them in developing collegial skills in order to build professional support networks that extend beyond the mentor?* <br><br> ➤ *Are teachers involved in teacher-led learning communities organized around ongoing collaborative inquiry that leads to instructional improvement in their schools? If not, how can we support site administrators in beginning or improving teacher-led learning communities?* <br><br> ➤ *Are new teachers being integrated into existing teacher-led learning teams in ways that will support new teacher learning and meaningful collaboration with colleagues? If not, what can mentors do to help with this transition?* <br><br> ➤ *If teacher-led learning teams do not exist in a school, could mentors develop professional learning teams for groups of* | |

*(continued)*

| | | |
|---|---|---|
| | *new teachers focused on context, content, or other common experiences that will help new teachers network with each other and learn the skills needed to be members of a professional community? How could these new teacher learning communities serve as models for what whole school professional learning communities could look like?* | |
| **New teachers are purposefully connected with a professional learning community that extends beyond their grade level, school, or district that supports teachers' individualized needs for ongoing professional learning.** | Connecting with professional colleagues beyond the school to improve teaching and learning: <br> ➢ *How are program leaders and mentors working with site and district leaders to learn about professional learning opportunities that connect with school and new teacher's individual learning goals such as district-wide professional development, subject-matter conferences, and online professional networks? How might they work together to find ways to make these doable options that can expand the professional knowledge and network of the new teacher?* | |

| C. Deepening Mentor-Administrator Connections | | |
|---|---|---|
| **Successful Implementation** | **Questions to Consider** | **Ideas Generated for Program Development** |
| **Mentors, program leaders, and site-based administrators meet regularly to learn about and discuss issues related to new teacher development, school goals, and integration of new teacher support into school systems and structures.** | ➢ *How can mentors and induction program leaders help site administrators understand and respect the role of the mentor?* <br><br> ➢ *How can mentors and site administrators explain the importance of the confidential relationship between mentor and new teacher and the need to respect that confidentiality?* <br><br> ➢ *How can mentors and induction program leaders explain the need for and support site administrators in clearly communicating value for induction, mentoring, and ongoing professional* | |

*(continued)*

|  | *learning to their staff?* |  |
|  | ➤ *How often are mentors and induction program leaders communicating and meeting with administrators? With administrators and new teachers together? Is this sufficient?* |  |
|  | ➤ *How might mentors and induction program leaders using their time with site administrators to learn about and align/integrate induction and mentoring with school priorities, structures and systems?* |  |
|  | ➤ *How might mentors and induction program leaders using their time with site administrators to discuss and problem solve issues related to new teacher development (both individual new teachers as well as beginning teachers in general?)* |  |
|  | ➤ *Who else is tasked with supporting new teachers in our school or district? How might we communicate with them? How might we consolidate or otherwise organize supports for new teachers so they are not overwhelmed?* |  |

| **D. Fostering Positive New Teacher-Administrator Relationships** | | |
| **Successful Implementation** | **Questions to Consider** | **Ideas Generated for Program Development** |
| Site administrators work to develop relationships with new teachers early in the year, help them set appropriate goals, and provide timely, positive, and useful feedback related to their progress towards those goals. | ➤ Do all schools provide an orientation run by the site administration? Does this meet the needs of new teachers? <br><br> ➤ Do new teachers at each school feel they have a strong working relationship with their site administrator? What are some elements of this positive relationship? How are successful site administrators developing these relationships? <br><br> ➤ What might manageable but rigorous |  |

(*continued*)

|  | goals for new teacher development aligned with teaching standards, school instructional goals, and the professional interests/needs of the new teacher look like? How might mentors and induction program leaders support site administrators in meeting with new teachers early in the year to set manageable but rigorous goals? How might mentors be involved in such discussions? |  |
|  | ➢ How much time are administrators spending in new teachers' classrooms both formally and informally observing and giving feedback? How might mentors and induction program leaders encourage site administrators in conducting regular goal-focused formative observation and feedback sessions (pre-conference, observation, post-conference) to examine new teacher's observational data, instructional practice and student work in relation to their goals? How might mentors be involved in such interactions? |  |
|  | ➢ How often do site administrators attend new teacher professional development sessions? How might mentors and induction program leaders encourage site administrators to attend these sessions? |  |

# Conclusion:
# Bringing It All Together

Every child deserves an expert teacher: one who knows and loves her content and how to teach it to students; who knows and cares about each of his students; one who can set goals for herself and continually question, think, problem solve, persist in seeking better ways of teaching; continue to grow her professional knowledge throughout her career; and who can collaborate with others in meaningful ways. We need these teachers to stay beyond their first few years so they can become truly excellent at what they do so that all students have the chance to learn from their experience.

To become this kind of passionate and thoughtful educator, teachers need support and guidance, particularly in the early phases of their career as they transition from teacher education into their own classrooms.

They need knowledgeable and well-trained mentors who know their content and their context and have the time in their jobs to help them learn these habits of mind. They need school administrators who understand the challenges new teachers face, who get to know them, who provide them with individualized support as well as meaningful collaboration time with their colleagues. They also need schools and districts that invest in creating comprehensive teacher professional development pipelines that can fully support teachers from teacher education through induction, and throughout their careers as educators.

Without these things in place, new teachers, especially the brightest and most ambitious ones, will find reasons to leave teaching at shockingly rapid rates that cost schools and districts dearly, not only in terms of dollars but also in student learning.

## WHAT SCHOOLS AND DISTRICTS CAN DO
## TO MAKE MENTORING WORK

What keeps good teachers in the profession are meaningful, structured, sustained, intensive professional development programs that allow new teachers to collaborate and observe expert others, to be observed by others, and to be part of networks or study groups in which all teachers share together, grow together, and learn to respect each other's work.

A district's priorities, and their decisions about the setup and content of a mentoring program, have a great deal to do with the effectiveness of that program. The most effective mentoring program leaders will:

1. *Carefully select, train, and use mentors' valuable skills and knowledge to support new teacher success.* Mentoring program success turns on the quality and successful utilization of its mentors. Careful decisions need to be made about how and by whom mentors are recruited and selected and the criteria for their selection. Those new mentors need carefully planned, rigorous, and ongoing professional development to ensure they can move new teachers as far and as fast as possible. Mentors need to be matched with new teachers in ways that will best use their knowledge and skills and be given a job and case load that allows them to spend the time necessary to sufficiently support each new teacher. Districts must make decisions such as:

   • whether mentors are chosen or assigned
   • the amount of training and support mentors receive
   • whether the mentor teaches the same subject or grade level as the novice
   • the mentor's accessibility to novices (i.e., whether they are located in the same building or are rotated in to the building regularly)
   • the frequency of contact between mentor and novice

   The way districts go about making these choices has a dramatic impact on the success of the mentoring program in general.

2. *Tailor support to match the diverse needs and strengths of new teachers.* New teachers are not a homogenous group. They come with a wide range of strengths and experiences that impact what they need from their mentors and how that support should be organized. They need a program tailored to focus on different parts of the teaching and learning process on a time line that is appropriate for them and in a way that is individualized, personalized, and contextualized. A one-size-fits-all approach will not work. To build a flexible mentoring program, districts need to consider:

- what new teachers bring to teaching. What do they know? What are they ready for? What do they need?
- what the standards are for teacher excellence. What do we expect new teachers to know and be able to do? How can mentors and new teachers set goals together that will lead to quick gains for both new teachers and their students?
- how we can support mentors in having a deep and flexible kit of process tools that they can use to create an individualized and contextualized mentoring experience for each new teacher.

3. *Work in coordination with school-based leaders to create a working environment conducive to new teacher success.* Mentors and program leaders know that even the best mentor with the best training cannot make up for untenable working conditions. Mentors need to support site and district administrators in creating teaching assignments that are sustainable for new teachers. They need to help administrators to plan schedules that allow both new and veteran teachers to plan and learn together in meaningful ways both within and across departments, schools, and districts. They need to build strong partnerships with site administrators to align supports for new teachers, and they need to support site administrators in developing strong and open working relationships with new teachers that help new teachers feel supported and cared for. When planning mentoring programs, districts need to consider:

- how new teachers are assigned to schools and districts
- how school schedules are developed to allow for collaboration both within and across schools
- how to educate principals about mentoring and develop aligned and integrated systems of support for new teachers
- how to educate principals about goal setting, feedback, and developing supportive relationships, particularly with new staff

It is also important for schools and districts to remember that mentoring alone is not enough to fully support new teachers. Induction is a comprehensive, multiyear process designed to train and acculturate new teachers into the academic standards and vision of a district that must be part of a seamless and sustained pipeline of professional support that extends from preservice through retirement in order to be truly effective. Fullan reminds us that sustained success is never just one special event, meeting, or activity; rather, it is a journey of recursive decisions and actions.[1]

The bottom line is that good teachers make the difference. Knowledgeable teachers with good habits of mind are effective teachers. When schools and districts provide structured, sustained support for their new teachers through mentoring, induction, and comprehensive professional development, they achieve what every school and district seeks to achieve—a more stable and better-prepared teaching force capable of tackling the enormous task of improving student learning.

## NOTE

1. Michael Fullan, *Leading in a Culture of Change*. San Francisco: Jossey-Bass, 2007.

# References

Abrams, Jenifer and Valerie Von Frank, *The Multigenerational Workplace: Communicate, Collaborate and Create Community*. Thousand Oaks, CA: Corwin, 2014.

Achinstein, Betty, "New Teacher and Mentor Political Literacy: Reading, Navigating, and Transforming Induction Contexts," *Teachers and Teaching: Theory and Practice* 12, no. 2, (2006): 123–138.

Achinstein, Betty and Steven Z. Athanases, eds. *Mentors in the Making: Developing New Leaders for New Teachers*. New York: Teachers College Press, 2006.

Achinstein, Betty and Steven Z. Athanases, "Mentoring New Teachers for Equity and the Needs of English Language Learners," In *Past, Present and Future Research on Teacher Induction: An Anthology for Researchers, Policy Makers, and Practitioners*, edited by Jian Wang, Sandra Odell and Renee Clift, 187–204. Commission on Teacher Induction and Mentoring, Association of Teacher Educators: Rowman & Littlefield Education.

Alliance for Excellent Education, *Tapping the Potential: Retaining and Developing High-Quality New Teachers*. Washington, DC: Author, 2004.

Ashton, Patricia, "Teacher efficacy: A Motivational Paradigm for Effective Teacher Education," *Journal of Teacher Education* 35, no. 5 (1984): 28–32.

Bandura, Alfred, "Social Cognitive Theory: An Agentic Perspective," *Annual Review of Psychology* 52 (2001): 1–26.

Barrett, K., Hovde, K., Hahn, Z. L., & Rosqueta, K. (2011). *High Impact Philanthropy to Improve Teaching Quality: Focus on High-Need Secondary Students*. Philadelphia, PA: Center for High Impact Philanthropy at University of Pennsylvania.

Ball, Deborah L. and David K. Cohen, "Developing Practice, Developing Practitioners: Toward a Practice-Based Theory of Professional Education. In *Teaching as the Learning Profession: Handbook of Policy and Practice*, edited by Gary Sykes and Linda Darling-Hammond, 3–32. San Francisco: Jossey Bass, 1999.

Boyd, Donald J., Pam Grossman, Hamilton Lankford, Susanna Loeb, and Jim Wyckoff, "How Changes in Entry Requirements Alter the Teacher Workforce and Affect Student Achievement," *Education Finance and Policy* 1, no. 2 (2006): 176–216.

Boyd, Donald J., Pam Grossman, Karen Hammerness, Hamilton Lankford, Susanna Loeb, Matthew Ronfeldt, and Jim Wyckoff, "Recruiting Effective Math Teachers: Evidence From New York City," *American Educational Research Journal* 49, no. 6 (2012): 1008–1047.

Breaux, Annette and Harry Wong, *New Teacher Induction: How to Train, Support and Retain New Teachers*. Mountain View, CA: Harry K. Wong Publications, 2003.

Bull, Barry L., Mark Buechler, Steve Didley and Lee Krehbiel, "Professional Development and Teacher Time: Principles, Guidelines, and Policy Options for Indiana." Bloomington, IN: Indiana Education Policy Center, School of Education, Indiana University, 1994.

Commission on Teacher Credentialing, "California Standards for the Teaching Profession (CSTP)." Sacramento, CA: 2009.

Cambone, Joseph, "Time for Teachers in School Restructuring," *Teachers College Record* 96, no. 3 (1995): 512–43.

Classroom Assessment Scoring System (CLASS). Charlottesville, VA: Teachstone

Coggins, Celine and Heather Peske, "New Teachers Are the New Majority," *Education Week*. (2011, January 19). Accessed from www.edweek.org/ew/articles/2011/01/19/17coggins.h30.html.

Coggins, Celine, "Holding on to Generation Y," *Educational Leadership* 67, no. 8 (2010): 70–74.

Cohen, Benjamin A. and Edward J. Fuller, "Effects of Mentoring and Induction on Beginning Teacher Retention." Paper presented at the Annual Meeting of the American Educational Research Association, San Francisco, CA, April 2006.

Corcoran, Tom C. "Transforming Professional Development for Teachers: A Guide for State Policymakers." Washington, D. C.: National Governors' Association, 1995.

Council of Chief State School Officers, *Interstate Teacher Assessment and Support Consortium (InTASC) Model Core Teaching Standards: A Resource for State Dialogue*. Washington, D.C.: Author, April 2011. Retrieved from: http://www.ccsso.org/Resources/Publications/InTASC_Standards_At_a_Glance_2011.html.

Danielson, Charlotte, "Revisiting Teacher Learning: A Framework for Learning to Teach," *Educational Leadership* 66 (June 2009). Accessed from: www.ascd.org/publications/educational-leadership/summer09/vol66/num09/A-Framework-for-Learning-to-Teach.aspx.

Danielson, Charlotte, *Enhancing Professional Practice: A Framework for Teaching*. Alexandria, VA: ASCD, 2007.

Darling-Hammond, Linda, Ruth Chung and Fred Frelow, "Variation in Teacher Preparation How Well Do Different Pathways Prepare Teachers to Teach?" *Journal of Teacher Education* 53, no. 4(2002): 286–302.

Darling-Hammond, Linda, Ruth Chung Wei, and Christy Marie Johnson, "Teacher Preparation and Teacher Learning: A Changing Policy Landscape," in *Handbook of Education Policy Research*, edited by Gary Sykes, Barbara L.

Schneider, and David N. Plank, 613–636. New York: American Educational Research Association and Routledge, 2009.

Davis, Emily, "Trust, Triage, and Teaching: Exploring Interactions Between Mentors and First-Year Teachers." PhD diss., University of Virginia, 2010.

Desimone, Laura, "Improving Studies of Teacher's Professional Development: Toward Better Conceptualizations and Measures," *Educational Researcher* 38, no. 3 (April 2009): 181–199.

Durham Mentoring Program, *How We Did It: The Process of Incorporating a Fulltime Mentoring Program in Durham Public Schools*. Unpublished manuscript, 2007.

Eccles, Jacquelynne S. and Allan Wigfield, "Motivational Beliefs, Values, and Goals," *Annual Review of Psychology* 53, no.1 (2002): 109–132.

Fantilli, Robert D. and Douglas E. McDougall, "A Study of Novice Teachers: Challenges and Supports in the First Years," *Teaching and Teacher Education* 25, no. 6 (2009): 814–825.

Feiman-Nemser, Sharon, "Helping Novices Learn to Teach: Lessons From an Exemplary Support Provider" *Journal of Teacher Education* 52, no.1 (2001): 17–30.

Feiman-Nemser, Sharon, "Teacher Mentoring: A Critical Review," *ERIC Digest* 95, no. 2 (July 1996). Accessed from: http://eric.ed.gov/?id=ED397060.

Feiman-Nemser, Sharon, "What New Teachers Need to Learn," *Educational Leadership* 60, no. 8 (2003): 25–29.

Feiman-Nemser, Sharon, Cynthia L. Carver, Daniel S. Katz and Sharon Schwille, *New Teacher Induction: Programs, Policies, Practices*. Final Report. East Lansing, MI, 1999.

Feiman-Nemser, Sharon and Margaret Buchmann, "When is Student Teaching Teacher Education?" *Teaching and Teacher Education* 3, no. 4 (1987): 255–273.

Feiman-Nemser, Sharon and Michelle B. Parker, "Making Subject Matter Part of the Conversation in Learning to Teach," *Journal of Teacher Education* 41, no. 3 (1990): 32–43.

Fletcher, Stephen H., Michael Strong, and Anthony Villar, "An Investigation of the Effects of Variations in Mentor-Based Induction on the Performance of Students in California," *Teachers College Record* 110, no. 10 (2008): 2271–2289.

Fidishun, Delores, "Andragogy and Technology: Integrating Adult Learning Theory As We Teach Technology," *Proceedings of the 2000 Mid-South Instructional Technology Conference*. Murfreesboro, TN: Middle Tennessee State University, April 2000. Accessed from: http://frank.mtsu.edu/~itconf/proceed00/fidishun .htm.

Fisher, Doug, "Close Reading of Complex Texts," Presentation to the Santa Cruz/ Silicon Valley New Teacher Project and the Santa Clara County Office of Education. San Jose, CA, January 25, 2014.

Fogo, Brad, "Secondary History Core Teaching Practices: Delphi Study Final Results." Stanford, CA: Center to Support Excellence in Teaching (October 2012). Accessed from: https://cset.stanford.edu/research/core-practices.

Fullan, Michael, *Leading in a Culture of Change*. San Francisco: Jossey-Bass, 2007.

Fuller, Edward J., "Do Properly Certified Teachers Matter? Properly Certified Algebra Teachers and Algebra I Achievement in Texas." Paper presented at the annual meeting of the American Educational Research Association, New Orleans, LA, April 2000.

Fuller, Edward J., *Beginning Teacher Retention Rates for TxBESS Teachers.* Unpublished manuscript, State Board for Educator Certification, Austin, Texas, 2003.

Ganser, Tom, "The New Teacher Mentors: Four Trends That Are Changing the Look of Mentoring Programs for New Teachers." *American School Board Journal* 189, no. 12 (2002): 25–27.

Garet, Michael S., Andrew C. Porter, Laura Desimone, Beatrice F. Birman, and Kwang Suk Yoon, "What Makes Professional Development Effective? Results From a National Sample of Teachers," *American Educational Research Journal* 38, no. 4 (Winter 2001): 915–945.

Glazerman, Steven, Eric Isenberg, Sarah Dolfin, Martha Bleeker, Amy Johnson, Mary Grider, and Matthew Jacobus, "Design of an Impact Evaluation of Teacher Induction Programs" (Final Report No. 6137-070). Washington, DC: Mathematica Policy Research, June 2010. Accessed from: http://www.math ematicampr.com/publications/redirect_PubsDB.asp?strSite=PDFs/education/ teacherinduction-fnlrpt.pdf.

Gold, Yvonne. "Beginning Teacher Support: Attrition, Mentoring, and Induction." *Handbook of Research on Teacher Education* 2, edited by John Sikula, T. Buttery, and E. Guyton, 548–594. New York: Macmillan, 1996.

Goldrick, Liam, David Osta, Dara Barin, and Jennifer Burn "Review of State Policies on Teacher Induction." Santa Cruz, CA: New Teacher Center, February 2012.

Grossman, Pamela and Emily Davis, "Mentoring That Fits," *Educational Leadership* 69, no. 8 (May 2012): 54–57.

Grossman, Pamela and Morva McDonald, "Back to the Future: Directions for Research in Teaching and Teacher Education," *American Educational Research Journal* 45, no. 1 (2008): 184–205.

Grossman, Pamela, Susanna Loeb, Jeannie Myung, Donald Boyd, Hamilton Lankford and James Wyckoff, "Learning to Teach in New York City: How Teachers and Schools Jointly Determine the Implementation of a District-Wide Mentoring Program," *National Society for the Study of Education Yearbook.* New York: Teachers College, Columbia University, 2012.

Gschwend, Laura, (former director of the Santa Cruz/Silicon Valley New Teacher Project) in conversation with the author, November, 2013.

Guskey, Thomas R. "Professional Development in Education: In Search of the Optimal Mix." Paper presented at the Annual Meeting of the American Educational Research Association, New Orleans, LA, 1994.

Hammerness, Karen, Linda Darling-Hammond, John Bransford, David Berliner, Marilyn Cochran-Smith, Morva McDonald, and Kenneth Zeichner (2005). "How Teachers Learn and Develop," in *Preparing Teachers for a Changing World: What Teachers Should Learn And Be Able To Do*, edited by Linda Darling-Hammond and John Bransford, 358–389. San Francisco: Jossey-Bass, 2005.

Hirsch, Eric, "Cross-State Analyses of Results of 2012–13 Teaching Empowering Leading and Learning (TELL) Survey." Santa Cruz, CA: New Teacher Center, 2013. Accessed from: http://www.newteachercenter.org/products-and -resources/teaching-and-learning-conditions-reports/cross-state-analyses -results-2012-13.

Ingersoll, Richard M., "The Teacher Shortage: A Case of Wrong Diagnosis and Wrong Prescription. *NASSP Bulletin* 86, no. 631 (2002): 16–31.

Ingersoll, Richard M. and Lisa Merrill, "Seven Trends: The Transformation of the Teaching Force," Research report published by the Consortium for Policy Research in Education (CPRE), 2012. Accessed from: http://www.cpre.org/7trends.

Ingersoll, Richard M. and Thomas M. Smith, "Do Teacher Induction and Mentoring Matter?" *NASSP Bulletin, 88*, no. 638 (2004): 28–40.

Isenberg, Eric, Steven Glazerman, Martha Bleeker, Amy Johnson, Julieta Lugo-Gil, Mary Grider, Sarah Dolfin and Edward Britton, "Impacts of Comprehensive Teacher Induction: Results from the Second Year of a Randomized Controlled Study. NCEE 2009-4072. *National Center for Education Evaluation and Regional Assistance,* 2009.

Isenberg, Eric, Steven Glazerman, Amy Johnson, Sarah Dolfin, and Martha Bleeker, "Linking Induction to Student Achievement," In *Past, Present and Future Research on Teacher Induction,* edited by Jian Wang, Sandra J. Odell, and Renee T. Clift, 221–240. New York: Rowman & Littlefield, 2010.

Johnson, Susan Moore and Susan M. Kardos, "Keeping New Teachers in Mind," *Educational Leadership* 59, no. 6 (2006): 13–16.

Johnson, Susan Moore, Susan M. Kardos, David Kauffman, Edward Liu, and Morgaen L. Donaldson, "The Support Gap: New Teachers' Early Experiences in High-Income and Low-Income Schools," *Education Policy Analysis Archives* 12 (2004): 61.

Kalogrides, Demetra, Susanna Loeb, and Tara Beteille "Systematic Sorting: Teacher Characteristics and Class Assignments, "*American Sociological Association: Sociology of Education* 86, no. 2 (2013): 103–123.

Kapadia, Kavita, Vanessa Coca, and John Q. Easton, "Keeping New Teachers: A First Look at the Influences of Induction in the Chicago Public Schools." University of Chicago: UChicago Consortium on Chicago School Research, 2007. Accessed from: http://ccsr.uchicago.edu/publications/keeping-new-teachers -first-look-influences-induction-chicago-public-schools.

Kardos, Susan M. and Susan M. Johnson, "On Their Own and Presumed Expert: New Teachers' Experience With Their Colleagues," *Teachers College Record* 109, no. 9 (2007): 2083–2106.

Knight, Jim, "Instructional Coaching: What We Are Learning About Effective Coaching Practices," Presentation to the National Staff Development Conference, Orlando, Florida, December 6, 2008.

Knowles, Malcolm S., *The Modern Practice of Adult Education: From Pedagogy to Andragogy.* Englewood Cliffs: Prentice Hall/Cambridge, 1980.

Knowles, Malcolm S., Elwood F. Holton III, and Richard A. Swanson, *The Adult Learner.* New York: Routledge, 2012.

Lehman, Paul R., "Ten Steps to School Reform at Bargain Prices," *Education Week* 23, no.13 (November 26 2003): 36, 28.

Lipton, Laura, Bruce Wellman, and Carlette Humbard, *Mentoring Matters: A Practical Guide to Learning-Focused Relationships.* Charlotte, VT: MiraVia, LLC, 2003.

Lortie, Dan, *Schoolteacher: A Sociological Study.* London: University of Chicago Press, 1975.

Lucas, Tamara and Jamie Grinberg, "Responding to the Linguistic Reality of Mainstream Classrooms: Preparing All Teachers to Teach English Language Learners. *Handbook of Research on Teacher Education: Enduring Questions in Changing Contexts* 3 (2008): 606–636.

Little, Judith W., "Understanding Data Use Practice Among Teachers: The Contribution of Micro-Process Studies," *American Journal of Education* 118, no. 2 (2012): 143–166.

Luft, Julie A. "Beginning Secondary Science Teachers in Different Induction Programmes: The First Year of Teaching," *International Journal of Science Education* 31, no. 17 (2009): 2355–2384.

Luft, Julie A. and Nancy C. Patterson, "Bridging the Gap: Supporting Beginning Science Teachers," *Journal of Science Teacher Education* 13, no. 4 (2002): 267–282.

Luft, Julie A., Gillian H. Roehrig, and Nancy C. Patterson, "Contrasting Landscapes: A Comparison of the Impact of Different Induction Programs on Beginning Secondary Science Teachers' Practices, Beliefs, and Experiences," *Journal of Research in Science Teaching* 40, no. 1 (2003): 77–97.

Madison Metropolitan School District, "Classroom Action Research," Madison, WI: Author, 2010. Accessed from: http://oldweb.madison.k12.wi.us/sod/car/carhomepage.html.

Malarkey, Tom, "Inquiry for Equity: What Does it Mean for Teacher Research?" In *Working Toward Equity* edited by Linda Friedrich, Carol Tateishi, Tom Malarkey, Elizabeth R. Simons and Marty Williams, 11–21. Berkeley, CA: National Writing Project, 2006.

Maisel, Josh (Fremont Union High School District Induction Program Director) in conversation with the author, January 2014.

MetLife, "The MetLife Survey of the American Teacher: Challenges for School Leadership," New York: Metropolitan Life Insurance Company, 2013. Accessed from: https://www.metlife.com/teachersurvey.

Michigan Department of Education ASSIST Program for New Teachers, "Selecting and assigning mentors," Lansing, MI: Author, 2013. Accessed from: http://assist.educ.msu.edu/ASSIST/school/principal/workbegintchrs/toolmentorselection.htm.

Mizelll, Hayes, "Why Professional Development Matters," *Learning Forward*, Oxford, OH: 2010. Accessed from:http://www.learningforward.org/docs/pdf/why_pd_matters_web.pdf.

Moir, Ellen, "Keynote Address," Presented at the Annual New Teacher Symposium, San Jose, CA, 2013.

Moir, Ellen, "Op-Ed: For First Year Teachers, It's Sink or Swim," *Take Part*, September 10, 2012. Accessed from: http://www.takepart.com/article/2012/09/10/first-year-teachers-its-sink-or-swim).

Moir, Ellen, Barlin, D., Janet Gless, and Jan Miles, *New Teacher Mentoring: Hopes and Promises for Improving New Teacher Mentoring*. Cambridge, MA: Harvard Education Press, 2009.

Mullinix, Bonnie B. "Selecting and Retaining Teacher Mentors," ERIC Clearinghouse on Teaching and Teacher Education, Washington, D. C., 2002. Accessed from: www.casenex.com/casenex/ericReadings/SelectingAndRetaining.pdf.

National Academy of Sciences, *Toward Understanding Teacher Supply and Demand.* Washington, DC: National Academy Press, 1987.

National Board for Professional Teaching Standards *Take One!* Arlington, VA: Author, 2013. Accessed from: http://www.nbpts.org/.

National Commission on Excellence in Education, "A Nation at Risk: The Imperative for Educational Reform," *The Elementary School Journal* 84, no. 2 (November 1983): 113–130.

National Commission on Teaching and America's Future, *No Dream Denied: A Pledge to America's Children.* Washington, D. C.: Author, 2003. Accessed from: www.nctaf.org.

National Commission on Teaching and America's Future, *Policy Brief: The High Cost of Teacher Turnover.* Washington, D. C.: Author, 2007. Accessed from: www.nctaf.org.

National Commission on Teaching and America's Future, *Who Will Teach? Experience Matters.* Washington, D. C.: Author, 2010. Accessed from: www.nctaf.org.

National Academy Press, *National Science Education Standards.* Washington, D. C.: Author, 1996.

New Teacher Center, *Mentor Selection.* Santa Cruz, CA: Author, 2011. Accessed from: bcmentoringnetwork.files.wordpress.com/2011/.../mentor-selection-ntc.pdf.

New Teacher Center, *State Policy Reviews.* Santa Cruz, CA: Author, 2014. Accessed from: http://www.newteachercenter.org/policy/policy-map.

North Carolina Department of Public Instruction, *North Carolina Mentor Teacher's Handbook: Activities and Tools for Supporting Beginning Teachers.* Raleigh, NC: Author, 2007.

Norton, M. Scott, "Teacher Retention: Reducing Costly Turnover," *Contemporary Education* 70, no. 3 (1999): 52–55.

Odell, Sandra J. and Douglas P. Ferraro, "Teacher Mentoring and Teacher Retention," *Journal of Teacher Education* 43, no. 3 (1992): 200–204.

Portner, Hall, *Training Mentors Is Not Enough: Everything Else Schools and Districts Need To Do.* Thousand Oaks, CA.: Corwin Press, 2001.

Robinson, Gary W. "New Teacher Induction: A Study of Selected New Teacher Induction Models and Common Practices." Paper presented at the annual meeting of the Midwestern Educational Research Association. Chicago, IL, October 1998.

Rockoff, Jonah E., "Does Mentoring Reduce Turnover and Improve Skills of New Employees? Evidence from Teachers in New York City" (Working Paper 13868). Cambridge, MA: National Bureau of Economic Research, 2008. Accessed from: www.nber.org/papers/w13868.

Rowe, Ken, "The Importance of Teacher Quality as a Key Determinant of Students' Experiences and Outcomes of Schooling," Paper presented at the ACER Research Conference (Building Teacher Quality: What Does The Research Tell Us?). Melbourne, Australia: October 19–21, 2003. Accessed from: http://www.acer.edu.au/research/programs/learningprocess.html.

Sandberg, Sheryl, *Lean In: Women, Work, and the Will to Lead.* New York: Random House, 2013.

Sapphire, Jonathan, Susan Freedman and Barbara Aschheim, *Beyond Mentoring: How to Nurture, Support, and Retain New Teachers*. Newton, MA: Teachers 21, 2001.

Schlechty, Phillip C., *Schools for the Twenty-First Century: Leadership Imperatives for Educational Reform*. San Francisco, CA: Jossey-Bass Inc., 1990.

Shields, Patrick M., Camille E. Esch, Daniel C. Humphrey, Viki M. Young, Margaret Gaston and Harvey Hunt, "The Status of the Teaching Profession: Research Findings and Policy Recommendations. A Report to the Teaching and California's Future Task Force." *The Center for the Future of Teaching and Learning*, Santa Cruz, CA: 1999.

Shulman, Lee S., "Knowledge and Teaching: Foundations of the New Reform," *Harvard Educational Review* 57, no. 1 (1987): 1–23.

Shulman, Lee S., *The Wisdom of Practice: Essays on Teaching, Learning, and Learning to Teach*. San Francisco: Jossey-Bass, 2004.

Smith, Thomas and Richard Ingersoll, "What Are The Effects of Induction and Mentoring on Beginning Teacher Turnover?" *American Educational Research Journal* 41, no. 3 (2004): 681–714.

Snyder, Thomas D., Sally A. Dillow, and Charlene M. Hoffman, "Digest of Educational Statistics, 2008." National Center for Educational Statistics, March 2009. Accessed from: http://nces.ed.gov/pubsearch/pubsinfo.asp?pubid=200902.

Solis, Adela, "Mentoring New Teachers For First-Day, First-Year Success," *Intercultural Development Research Association Newsletter*, December 2009. Accessed from: http://www.idra.org/IDRA_Newsletter/November__December_2009_Student_Success/Mentoring_New_Teachers/#sthash.7gzgnyTe.dpuf.

Stanford History Education Group. *Reading Like A Historian*. Accessed from: http://sheg.stanford.edu/rlh.

Strong, Michael, "Does New Teacher Support Affect Student Achievement," *Research Brief # 06*, 1 (2006).

Strong, Michael, *Effective Teacher Induction and Mentoring: Assessing the Evidence*. New York: Teachers College Press, 2009.

Strong, Michael and Wendy Baron, "An Analysis of Mentoring Conversations With Beginning Teachers: Suggestions and Responses," *Teaching and Teacher Education* 20, no. 1 (2004): 47–57.

Strong, Michael and Linda St. John, *A Study of Teacher Retention: The Effects of Mentoring for Beginning Teachers*. Santa Cruz, CA: New Teacher Center, 2001.

Teoh, Mark, and Celine Coggins, "Great Expectations: Teachers' Views on Elevating the Profession. Boston: Teach Plus, 2013. Retrieved from www.teachplus.org/.

Texas Center for Educational Research, "The Cost of Teacher Turnover." Austin, TX: Texas Center for Educational Research, October 2000. Accessed from: www.tasb.org/about/related/tcer/.../17_teacher_turnover_full.pdf.

Thompson, Marnie, Pamela Paek, Laura Goe, and Eva Ponte, "Study of the California Formative Assessment and Support System for Teachers: Report 3, Relationship of BTSA/CFASST and Student Achievement (CFASST Rep. No. 3, ETS RR-04-32). Princeton, NJ: Educational Testing Service, 2004.

Tillman, B. A. "Quiet leadership: Informal Mentoring of Beginning Teachers," *Momentum* 31, no. 1 (2000): 24–6.

Troen, V., and K. Bolles, "Two Teachers Examine the Power of Teacher Leadership. In *Teachers as Leaders: Perspectives on the Professional Development of Teachers*, edited by D. R. Walling, 275–86. Bloomington, IN: Phi Delta Kappa Educational Foundation, 1994.

Veenman, Simon, "Perceived Problems of Beginning Teachers," *Review of Educational Research* 54, no. 2 (1984): 143–178.

Villani, Susan, *Mentoring Programs for New teachers: Models of Induction and Support*. Corwin Press, 2002.

Villar, Anthony and Michael Strong, "Is Mentoring Worth the Money? A Benefit-Cost Analysis and Five-Year Rate of Return of a Comprehensive Mentoring Program for Beginning Teachers," *ERS Spectrum* 25, no. 3 (2007): 1–17.

Walsh, K., and S. Jacobs, *Alternative Certification Isn't Alternative*. Washington, D.C.: Thomas B. Fordham Institute, 2007.

Wang, Jian and Sandra J. Odell, "Mentored Learning to Teach According to Standards-Based Reform: A Critical Review," *Review of Educational Research* 72, no. 3 (2002): 481–546.

Wang, Jian, Michael Strong and Sandra J. Odell, "Mentor-Novice Conversations About Teaching: A Comparison of Two U.S. and Two Chinese Cases. *Teacher College Record* 106, no. 4 (2004): 775–813.

Watts, G. D., and S. Castle, "The Time Dilemma in School Restructuring," *Phi Delta Kappan* 75, no. 4 (1993): 306–10.

Wechsler, Marjorie E., Kyra Caspary, Daniel C. Humphrey and Kavita K. Matsko, "Examining the Effects of New Teacher Induction." Menlo Park, CA: SRI International, 2010.

Wei, Ruth C., Linda Darling-Hammond, Aletha Andree, Nikole Richardson, Stelios Orphanos, "Professional Learning in the Learning Profession: A Status Report on Teacher Development in the United States and Abroad." Dallas, TX: National Staff Development Council, 2009.

Williams, Fred, (Former Durham, North Carolina Induction Program Director) in conversation with the author, January 2014.

Williams, Fred and Rhonda Stubin, "Program Accountability Supports Sustainability." Presentation at the New Teacher Annual Symposium, Burlingame, CA: February 2014. Burlingame, CA New Teacher Center Annual Symposium.

Wong, Harry K. "Induction Programs That Keep New Teachers Teaching and Improving," *NASSP Bulletin* 88, no. 638 (2004): 41–58.

Zeichner, Kenneth M. and Hilary G. Conklin, "Teacher Education Programs," in *Studying Teacher Education: The Report of the AERA Panel on Research and Teacher Education* edited by Marilyn Cohran-Smith and Kenneth M. Zeichner. Washington, D. C., 2005.